To: My friend,

# get a G.R.I.P.
### ...when it all falls apart

Phil 4: 6-9
Be anxious for nothing :...

Love, Becky Weeks
praying for you as you read
through the pages.

# get a G.R.I.P.
## ...when it all falls apart

## Beverly Weeks

FREEDOM FOX PRESS
Dancing Lemur Press, L.L.C.
Pikeville, North Carolina
www.dancinglemurpress.com

Copyright 2016 by Beverly Weeks
Published by Freedom Fox Press
An imprint of:
Dancing Lemur Press, L.L.C., P.O. Box 383,
Pikeville, North Carolina, 27863-0383
www.dancinglemurpress.com

ISBN: 9781939844170

Printed in the United States of America

Library of Congress Control Number: 2015959750

# Dedication

*I* want to dedicate the pages within this book to you, my friend. You see I realize that I may never know your name, but God does. I pray for anointing upon each word as you flip through the pages. I pray that God will touch the raw, hurting, secret places of your heart, and bring healing, wisdom, and hope for every desperate situation.

We may never meet, but I want you to know that I love you and have prayed for you, even before you opened the front cover. Always remember on the days that you are feeling unheard, unseen, and insignificant- God sees, He knows, and He cares.

No matter how complicated things seem, how grim things may look, when you want to give up, when people talk about you, cast you out, or even ridicule you... You are a beloved child of a Sovereign God....a God who is BIGGER than anything you may face.

Love,

Beverly Weeks

# Acknowledgements

*To Rick, Tyler & Macy: Thank you for always believing in me, that has made all the difference... I love you so very, very much.*

*To Mom, Dad, Debbie, Michelle & Sharon: Can you believe it? I wrote a book with the words ain't shain't, & gonna. Goes to prove God doesn't always call the qualified, but He will qualify the called!*

*To Scott & Sherry: Thank you for pushing me to be real, strive higher, pray harder & have fun.*

*To Jamie Cooper: Thank you for clearly catching the vision of my message.*

*To Bethany, Fifi, & Sheila: I could have never taken this journey without you.*

*To my friends at Wayne Pregnancy Care Center: Thank you for not kicking me out of the office when I asked you to join me on this journey. You have laughed with me, cried with me, and sometimes even shook your head in disbelief when I asked you to dream crazy BIG with me! I love you more than you will ever know. You all AMAZE me! I thank my God for each of you!*

*To Diane & the rest of the Freedom Fox Press publishing team: Thank you for your feedback, for processing every word & for your encouragement.*

*To my God: All the glory, honor and the praise belongs to you! Thank you for giving me the desires of my heart.*

# Table of Contents

# Foreword

**F**ather, my heart is heavy. I have friends reading this who are facing situations that just look grim. I sense that many of them are physically and mentally exhausted by their circumstance. Father God, I ask that you will give them DIVINE WISDOM in how to handle their finances, relationships, marriages, struggles with jobs, attacks of gossip, or any unknown certainties with their health. Lord, I ask that you will refresh their minds, command the depression to scatter, and give them a new HOPE!

In the name of Jesus, I command every evil conspiracy that has been planned by the enemy to be destroyed and roasted by the fire of God! Lord, I pray that you will order our steps, our thoughts, and every word that leaps from our tongue. Father, surround my friends with your presence and empower us all to do your will! Thank you for loving us more than anyone else ever could.

In your name we pray, Amen!

# Part I

# Get a G.R.I.P.

# Confession Time

*I*t's time for me to come clean. Time to lay it all out on the table, confess, disclose my well-kept hidden secret to the world, and come to grips with the unavoidable truth that I have an unpleasant, downright annoying, sinful habit.

I've always said that if there was a local weekly support group for this wide spread global addiction, I would reluctantly be the first to stand up to give my name. So here it goes my impromptu delayed introduction. My name is Beverly and, well, um... I am a member of Worryaholics Anonymous.

I've been known to worry about my kids, marriage, job, a doctor's diagnosis, the flip flopping numbers on my uncooperative bathroom scales, the depleting balance in our often drained checking account, past regrets, and a host of other concerns on my lengthy list. At times I have even struggled and shamelessly battled a debilitating, life draining disease that I call the *People Pleasing Syndrome!*

I know what it's like to toss and turn, to lie awake in bed at night because you just can't sleep. I've tasted salty tears as they rushed down the side of my cheeks after yelling out in frustration, *"God are you there? Are you even listening?"* I've experienced the pain of gossip, rejection, been walked out on, carried the weight of guilt, unforgiveness, and felt that sickening misery that lingers deep down in the pit of the stomach when you are attacked by what ifs, if onlys, and the whys of life, and you desperately want more than anything to experience some kind of peace.

In light of this admission, I think it's only fitting that I get candid with you about something.

Oh, I'm full tilt at speaking on worry and fear, all the while encouraging others. Yet I still recognize that the conflicted skirmish of negative thoughts within my own mind has always been a REAL battle.

I once read somewhere that the average person has an estimated 50 to 70 thousand thoughts running through their mind in a given day. Some days I suspect that I conjure up that many thoughts in a single hour!

Think about this: every single action that you do started with a thought. Our minds are in a constant battle with evil and good. There are days when the enemy tries to make me feel like a total failure; he attacks my mind and tells me I'm not smart enough, pretty enough, not qualified, and that I tee-totally FLUNK at motherhood, as a Christian, and as a wife.

In all honesty, if I am not careful, those thoughts can pull me into a dark pit of unexpected depression. A while back, I went to pick up my kids from school. It had been one of those *"I give up, I just want to QUIT!"* days in ministry. My overcommitted calendar and work at the crisis pregnancy care center had emotionally drained me. Among the schedule of appointments, was a meeting with a young teen-aged mom who had been raped.

Soon after finding out that she was pregnant, in an attempt to end her life and the life of her unborn child, this young girl had cut her arms multiple times with a razor blade.

She went on to explain to me how after the botched suicide attempt failed, she had thrown herself down a flight of stairs. The fear in her voice, jumbled together with all of her unknowns, cries for help, and my wanting to "fix it" personality, had left me numb.

As I approached the school car rider line, the enemy immediately began to have a fiasco with me, and pounced on my mind with negative thoughts. *You're not smart enough, not qualified, you've bombed as a mother, flopped as a wife, and you'll never amount to anything* began to resonate in my ears.

My teen-aged son opened the car door and leaped into the front seat, while my daughter rested in the back. At that moment, every single deep-rooted emotion I had compressed for what seemed like 20 years exploded and gushed out of my mouth.

Right there in the front seat of that 215,000 mile, compact clunkermobile, I had a momma meltdown and blurted out, *"I am so sorry! I have been a terrible mother! All the other moms on Facebook cook gourmet meals, biscuits, meatloaf, vegetables, and homemade pies. The closest I have come to that this week is hot dogs made with red dye number 40 and Fruit Loops for dessert.*

*"I'm just awful! On top of that, you're the only kids in line without monogrammed lunch boxes. You had to bring your sandwich in a grocery store plastic bag. I have failed!"* Tears went to falling and snot went to flying as I let all my frustrations and emotions ooze out.

Puzzled by my outburst, my son looked at me and said something along the lines of, *"Mom, get yourself together. Now is NOT a good time for you to have an emotional breakdown. We are in the car rider line and every girl's eyes are on me. You're gonna ruin my chances! Snap out of it mom. Get yourself together."*

All of us have been there. Your stories may not be quite as dramatic as mine. For some of you, the story is much worse. And for many of you, the fiery darts of fear are being launched at you right now.

Have you ever noticed that spiritual warfare conveniently attacks when you are exhausted, hungry, overcommitted with your schedule, rushed, or overwhelmed?

How about when you are hangry? (That's hungry and angry all mixed together.) You know what it's like to be assaulted with negative, pessimistic thinking, and to agonize with fear. You may even be walking out that season right now of those painful days and nights, which seem to go on for what feels like months.

Years ago, I walked out that fear and uncertainty in my marriage. Everything seemed so dark. I found myself tangled in an emotional affair, a web of deception, and living a life flirting with sin. My marriage was broken, and I no longer had the will, want, or desire to fix it. My mind became consumed with thoughts of bitterness and unforgiveness.

Over and over again I pondered the hurtful names that I had been called, the lack of communication, non-existent intimacy with my husband, and the cutting words spewed toward me in moments of anger after I purposely and arrogantly pushed all his buttons. I used it all to justify wanting to end my marriage.

**The Look of Hopelessness**

I could see the look of worry, fear, and doubt looming over my husband's thinning face. I tried to ignore it yet, I could sense his dire hopelessness. He refused to give up on our marriage. I remember looking out from the balcony of our church, Sunday after Sunday, as he would make his way to the altar during the invitation, drop to his knees weeping, crying out to God to restore our family. All the while, I would sit there unmoved by his emotions, still adamantly planning how to end the marriage so that we could both get on with our lives.

God miraculously restored and brought about divine healing in our marriage. My husband still shares with the couples we counsel how those days for him were filled with so much grief, uncertainty, and pain. For the first time in his life, he knew what it was like to feel that all hope was gone.

## Do You Feel All Hope Is Gone?

Maybe you are there now. You find yourself right smack dab in the middle of a blazing fire, a broken marriage, an ugly separation, a dispute with a teen-aged son or daughter, unresolved hurt from your past, a diagnosis of cancer, sickness, grief from the death of a loved one, or a struggle in your finances- the debt just keeps mounting and you cannot see any possible way out of your situation. Fear commands control of your mind, holding you captive while paralyzing you in its grasp.

A sure sign that life is unraveling is when worry hits you. Those times when it seems that all of hell is breaking loose and you can't seem to get a grip on life. I know all too well what it's like to walk into a church with my plastic, phony smile, acting as if I had it all together, yet deep inside I was dying and feeling as if my world was about to collapse.

## Some of Satan's Greatest Weapons are Psychological

*"The thief cometh not, but for to steal, and to kill, and to destroy..."* **John 10:10 (KJV)**

Do you understand that Satan wants to kill your hopes and dreams, destroy your family and relationships, bury your self-esteem, and crush you?

Think about it- he doesn't have to bind you with a rope to kill or destroy you.

Worry and fear are two of the enemy's most popular weapons he uses against us to steal our faith and keep us in bondage. Satan knowingly sets out to bombard your thoughts with worry which can make you physically sick, cause you to question God, be tormented with fear, and even filled with anxiety. Worry can lead to panic attacks, depression, make you doubt your self- worth. It can contribute to weight gain, headaches, and even provoke heart attacks.

*"I love God's law with all my heart. But there is another power within me that is at war with my mind. This power makes me a slave to sin that is still within me."* **Romans 7:22-23 (NLT)**

## Are you being attacked with paralyzing fear? HOLD ON!

My God has heard your moanings and your groanings and He has seen your tears! I remember my first year of church youth camp. I was excited to have my very own yellow and black polka dot bathing suit but even more thrilled to be swimming in the pool with the older girls.

18

They could flip and do awesome amazing tricks from the diving board. It was all I could do to keep my head afloat. The doggy paddle was the only swimming technique I had ever known. I ain't gonna lie to ya'll, it still is!

Here I found myself in a nine feet deep concrete swimming pool where my lack of experience was showing. I didn't dare allow the big girls to discover that I did not know how to swim.

Little by little, I would edge just a little bit closer to the drop off at the deep end of the pool, attempting to maintain the fake appearance of a skillful swimmer. I would hold on to the side, laugh, cut up with the others, and hope no one would ever suspect that I truly was a novice.

Then it happened! There was a large splash into the pool made by one of the adult swimmers, and it caused me to lose my footing. The water went right over my head and I slipped from the guardrail plummeting beneath all nine feet of water.

Paralyzed with fear, I began to panic and gasp for air. My heart raced, and thoughts of death crept into my young mind as the water rushed in through my nose and mouth. I began to tell myself, *"Kick! Just paddle back up to the surface."* The anxiety soon took over as I swallowed even more water. *"Kick, kick! You can do it! Kick yourself back up to the top."* Struggling, I mustered up enough strength, stretched out my arms and was able to paddle up to the top long enough to let out a loud scream for help.

At that moment, the lifeguard tossed one of those red and white life rings to me and a counselor jumped in to save me.

## Fear vanished in the arms of my rescuer!

What an overwhelming sense of relief to feel the arms of my rescuer so tightly around my waist and to know at that very moment, everything was going to be fine. More importantly to me, I was going to live!

There have been times in my adult life when I was crippled by that same gripping fear I experienced that day as a child. Life hit harder than I ever expected and I didn't know how I was going to make it or come back up to the surface.

How will we survive on one paycheck after I lost my job? How do I survive the doctor's diagnosis after finding a lump in my breast? How will I survive a crumbling marriage, or the grief from the sudden death of a loved one? It was during those times that I felt as if I was going under. That kind of fear will disrupt your life, drain all of your strength, and cloud your judgment. It's time to cry out, *"GOD, I FEEL LIKE I AM GOING UNDER! Help me! Toss me a life ring! Lord, I'm depending on you to save me."*

## You're Not Going Under!

I want you to know that our God did not give us a spirit of fear, but instead He has given us POWER and love to overcome those fears. Let's face it. We all experience times of uncertainty or difficulty.

Friends, there will be those days of rough waters, days when your very faith is fractured and shaken to the core, when you have to take hold of God's promises found in the Word, reach out to the one true Lifesaver, call on His name, go to kicking with all that is in you, and find rest in knowing that your Lifeguard walks on water. You can find safety in His arms. He loves you and I can assure you that my God is not about to let you go under.

*"Fear not for I am with you; Be not dismayed, for I am your God. I will strengthen you, Yes I will help you, I will uphold you with My righteous right hand."* Isaiah 41:10 (NKJV)

So what do you do when everything seems like it is falling apart? When demons have been unleashed and it feels like all of hell is breaking loose? When you are standing at the crossroads of despair, wondering which way to turn, and you find yourself giving up, giving in, or losing hope?

## Get A G.R.I.P.!!!!!!!!!!!!!!!!!!!!!

I remember as a young girl being picked on in school, and how my self-esteem was squashed. Someone had undoubtedly called me a name, made fun of my freckles, pony tails, long granny dress, or two front buckteeth, and I had come running into the classroom crying.

It was then that I was greeted by a hair-splitting phrase shouted out by one of my middle school classmates. A statement that used to jerk my jaw, yet it was spoken as a nonchalant way to calm me down. Three bold words... GET A GRIP! In other words, calm down, regain your composure, and pull yourself together.

In these next few pages, I want to get real with you and share four steps to renew your hope as we look at healing and taking authority over those dominating negative thoughts that have tormented your mind.

While you may not be able to stop a thought from entering your mind, you can control how long you dwell on it. Don't allow negative thoughts to take up space rent free in your mind. It's time to take a stand, plant your feet firmly on your spiritual stompin' grounds against that slimeball enemy, and shout out at the top of your lungs, *"NO WEAPON, and I mean absolutely, tee-totally NO WEAPON formed against me shall prosper! It won't work! Satan, you will NO longer have control over my thoughts."*

Right now, as you are reading this, I want you to believe and anticipate with me that God is going to do something so incredibly powerful and amazing in the situation or dilemma that you are facing, it will be life altering, mind boggling, earth rattling, and leave you in awe of the majestic power of God! I sense some HOLY SHIFTING is about to take place in your circumstance.

I want to say to you: *Get a G.R.I.P.! As long as you are breathing, there is hope.*

# G: Go to God in Prayer

*Y*ears ago, before our marriage fell apart, we rarely prayed together as a couple or a family, unless of course it was a hasty blessing over the food.

In all honesty, I don't really know why we never prayed together. Maybe it was because I was scared that my words wouldn't be good enough, or that I wouldn't have enough conviction in my voice for my words to reach God, let alone rattle the heavens in time of troubles. I was SO wrong!

God tells us in His word that we are to pray without ceasing, and ask for what we want in His name. You see, I have found that the power is NOT in my prayer life or any fancy words, but rather the power is found in praying to our GREAT BIG GOD! It is not about our might nor our power, BUT IT IS all about HIS spirit and HIS power! There are days that I pray with passion and I put my whole heart into it.

Yet, just being real, there have been recent days when grief, distress, and fear have overtaken me. It was all I could do just to muster up enough strength to cry out the name of JESUS!

I am so glad that God knows my heart, and even before a word leaps from my tongue He already knows my every concern. Friend, when you pray, pray with feeling, pray with a sense of urgency, get real with God, forget about the fancy words, pray kneeling, pray standing, pray in your car, at the stoplight, in the gym, in a closet, be silent, be loud, but above all, PRAY!

Did you know that prayer is one of our most POWERFUL weapons against spiritual warfare and trials?

*"Be anxious for nothing, but in everything by prayer and supplication, with thanksgiving, let your requests be made known to God; [7] and the peace of God, which surpasses all understanding, will guard your hearts and minds through Christ Jesus."* Philippians 4:6-7 New King James Version (NKJV)

Our God doesn't care as much about the words we say. He just wants to hear the moanings and groanings of our heart. I found out that there is no magic formula to prayer. Prayer is simply talking to God and pouring your heart out to him.

I've often heard people say that prayer changes ***things***. I like to say that prayer changes **YOU**, and then it gives you the courage to see things in a different light. Prayer gives you a whole new perspective!

## S.O.S. Prayers

*"You are kidding me right?"* It was not the kind of news I had prepared myself for when my boss called me into his office. In all honesty, working in commissioned sales had always proved to be a lucrative career for me. Yet I will admit, there were weeks when I walked on egg shells and lived in fear as I wondered where the next lead or closed contract would come from.

I sat there with my notebook and pen in hand as the owner explained that there would be some major changes made in the way I would be paid.

The adjustments and new policies would take effect immediately. I found myself in a very difficult place, and I had no choice but to resign from my position.

The drive on the way home was filled with fear and anxiety. *How would we survive on just one income? With all the talk of the slowing economy how would I ever find another job? What would my friends and family think of me?* I began to weep as I allowed the doubts and fear to take over my thoughts. My back was up against a wall, my family's financial security had been shaken, Satan was aggressive in his attack on me, and I felt completely worthless.

I knew that there was no way my situation could resolve itself. I was desperate, nervous, high strung, edgy, had financial obligations, and I felt as if my world was falling apart. I want you to know, I was just plain "scared to death!" Have you ever been there? I had no other recourse but to bury my face in my hands, drop to my knees, and cry out to GOD with what I call S.O.S. prayers.

I recognized I had limitations. I needed GOD and I needed Him to make haste to deliver, help, and save me! I felt as if I were drowning in my circumstances, yet I knew without a doubt that He would be my **SOURCE OF STRENGTH.** I recognized my God's ABILITY. **HE WAS ABLE**.

I knew He cared about the pain I was feeling and more importantly I **BELIEVED** in the power of prayer! Satan had set out to destroy my self-worth, and cause confusion in my life, family, and emotions. The attack seemed to be more than I could bear.

I got my imaginary white S.O.S. flag in hand and I went to waving it to the throne. *HELP, it's me! HELP! GOD,*

*You are my Father, I am standing on Your promises, and I need You to save me.*

Let me stop right here for a moment. Friend, did you know the word Father means *Source*? You heard me right. He is our source for healing, our source when we are in financial despair, our source when the marriage is broken, our source when that spouse has walked out, our source when that child's special needs are too much to handle, our source when we are being attacked by that gossip...**GOD IS OUR SOURCE!**

What burden are you carrying today that you just need to fall to your knees right now and shout out, *"S.O.S.! God be my SOURCE OF STRENGTH!"*

**"Come to me, all you who are weary and burdened, and I will give you rest. Take my yoke upon you and learn from me, for I am gentle and humble in heart, and you will find rest for your souls. For my yoke is easy and my burden is light."Matthew 11:28-30 (NIV)**

# R: Rally Your Support Team

**S**urround yourself with godly people and friends who will encourage you and hold you accountable.

I vaguely remember back in 2002, the story that came out of Pennsylvania where nine miners had been trapped for several days in frigid cold waters some 240 feet below the surface for nearly 77 hours.

What I loved about the story is that some time later after being rescued, the miners went on to describe how they survived. There were many times that one of them would feel like he was going under, like he could not hold on any longer. He would begin to panic and think he was going to die.

The other eight would huddle around him, doing everything they knew how to keep him warm. They would encourage him and offer words of hope until they felt like the miner's despair had passed.

I don't know about you, but there have been several times in my life where I felt like I just could not take it anymore. I am so glad that I had someone cheering me on, standing in the battle with me.

When all of hell breaks loose, and you feel like you are going under, when the pain is too much to bear, and you are feeling like you want to stop the world and get off, it's time to rally your support team.

## "Ain't Nothin' Like True Blue Cellulite Friends"

*"Girlfriend, I am saving you from the anguish! Don't you even attempt to wear those white pants. It's the end of September. Hang 'em up, your cellulite and red underwear are showing. You don't even need to go there!"*

Whew, thank goodness for "true blue cellulite friends." Never heard it quite expressed my way? Honey, everyone needs a couple of these confidants in their lives.

You know, the kind of friend that will let you know the hamburger is stuck in your front teeth and the chocolate ice cream residue is smeared on your mouth BEFORE you walk into a crowd to give a speech on self-esteem and eating healthy.

I love to take my friend Phyllis bathing suit shopping. She kills me with her candid responses, BUT she has saved me a lifetime of embarrassment!

*"Bev you just might want to try a bathing suit, with how should I say this politely.... a little skirt on the bottom?"* Honestly, I love it. She has got to be one of the greatest shopping buddies. *"Hmmm...those pants are slimming, but those are not, don't you think you're a little old for the JUNIOR department?"*

I have friends that are experts in the fake tanning department, *"Bev, you are looking rather ORANGE today, you trying a new spray?"* Then there are the accessories. Most of the time, you will find my jewelry and shoes match. They can't help but coordinate. Half the 'accessory police' live in my neighborhood. No kidding! Sometimes I cannot even get out of my driveway without someone issuing me a citation. I'm on probation now just for wearing scuffed up boots and out of style ear bobs.

We will not even go there with the looks my friends have given me in Zumba class. I just shout back, *"Don't say a word, can't you see my pants are SPLIT, I've fallen, and I can't get up!"*

Oh, but there is just something special about the spiritual accountability that godly friends can hold you to. Everyone needs a peer or mentor that they can trust to keep him or her accountable in his or her relationship with Christ, with their spouse, with an addiction, or any area where we are known to stumble.

That accountability is simply a check and balance system that protects us from harming others and ourselves.

My friend Sherry and I have such a bond. We confide, pray, listen, cry, laugh, and encourage each other. There have been touchy times in my marriage, finances, with my job, and even with my health when I did not need someone to necessarily solve the problem.... I just needed someone to listen. Often she would say, *"Bev, let's take a look and see what God says about this."*

**My first accountability is to my God.** The dearest most precious friend I have. Yet that accountability to another friend keeps me responsible for my actions. Do you have a confidant to whom you can go? Will that person truly hold you accountable in your spiritual walk or simply share the words you want to hear? If not, pray and begin to ask God to send someone (of the same gender) into your life to encourage and empower you.

You will find that when your world is turned upside

down and you just don't know how you are going to make it, there is nothing more precious than a godly friend. On occasion, I have to remind myself of how essential it is that I am *being* that kind of friend to others. Which kind of friend are you?

*"Therefore, confess your sins to each other and pray for each other so that you may be healed. The prayer of a righteous person is powerful and effective."* **James 5:16 (NIV)**

# I: Ignore Naysayers & Negative Thoughts

**W**ho are you listening to? I remember that time in my marriage years ago, when everything seemed as if it was going to crumble. There were people in my life I chose to listen to, and all they offered were words of discouragement and doubt. *"You can find better. Just let him go. You deserve to be happy."*

Be careful who you are seeking advice from. Are the words given lining up with the Word of God? I am here to tell you that the things whispered in your ear can make all the difference in your desire to succeed or fail, your desire to be healed, your desire to work on your marriage, your desire to be set free from the pit you have fallen into, and your desire to overcome this giant mountain facing you.

Naysayers can be found within your friends, family, and even within your church! During life, there seems to be that handful of critics who will not only tell you what you cannot do, but what you can't accomplish. I know what it's like to have words tossed at you like, *"You'll never amount to anything."* No matter what your challenge, there will be those around you who expect you to fail. Some may even desire it.

Satan wants to thwart your God-given purpose and he will stop at nothing to see that you are attacked with gossip, belittled, or assaulted with negative words. Whoever came up with the phrase, *"Sticks and stones may break my bones, but words will never hurt me"*

31

was way off target. Sometimes words can just about kill ya!!

While we are on the subject of negative words and naysayers, excuse me while I step all over my own hot pink, polka dot polished toes. I am going to need a pedicure by the time I finish! Ouch, here goes...

There was a time in my marriage when I would meet my husband at the side door just as he was arriving home from work, and I can assure you I wasn't standing there wrapped in a bow or eager to give him a kiss!

*"How was your..."* He could not even finish the question before I blurted it out. *"You're late, dinner is cold, Tyler wants new shoes, and when you fix the bed make sure you turn the pillow tags facing the back! Do you know how many calories you could burn by picking up your own towels?"*

Whew, talk about throwing a twenty-five pound bowling ball and hitting him in the gut. No doubt he wanted to grab his calculator, deadlines, and budgets and head straight back to that hospital, probably to get himself a room.

I have found that nagging words can kill romance, his self-esteem, AND disrupt family peace. Ladies, God calls us to be ENCOURAGERS! We need to be our husband's biggest cheerleader. Our words are to affirm the good, lift him up, and to bring out the very best in him.

Let's pray today that God will lead us to choose words of *grace*. Give me an R-I-C-K! What does it spell? RICK! GO RICK! Who's the handsomest hunk? RICK, GO RICK! Yay! Let's cheer for our spouse. We are on the same team! Oops, I got carried away. Let me see now, where is that old set of pom-poms...

*"Let no corrupting talk come out of your mouths, but only such as is good for building up, as fits the occasion, that it may give grace to those who hear."* **Ephesians 4:29 (ESV)**

**Ignoring the Negative Thoughts:**

**The more you think about, or fixate your mind on something, the stronger it will take hold of you.**

When a negative thought enters your mind, you have the ability to push it out of the mind and replace it with a godly thought. This verse says it all...

Finally, brethren, whatever things are true, whatever things *are* noble, whatever things *are* just, whatever things *are* pure, whatever things *are* lovely, whatever things *are* of good report, if *there is* any virtue and if *there is* anything praiseworthy—meditate on these things. Philippians 4:8 (NKJV)

# P: Prepare & Praise

*B*e ready and prepared for battle at all times! I'm not gonna lie, there have been many times that I have had to say, *God I need YOU to adjust MY attitude to that of gratitude.* The enemy would try to attack my mind and self-esteem and fill it with doubt, discouragement, and despair, and I lived in the pit of woe is me.

It is at those times that I have to take a deep breath, get a G.R.I.P., put on my armor and remind myself that I am an overcomer and speak God's Word out loud. My Bible tells me that the enemy hates this, so when I declare the promises of God by standing on His word, Satan and all his pathetic demons have to flee. Demons go to itching and a cringing!

In Philippians 4:13, I read that *I can do all things through Christ who strengthens me.* In Psalm 18:2, I am reminded that *the Lord is my Rock and my fortress and my deliverer. My God, my strength in whom I will trust; my shield and the horn of my salvation, my stronghold.*

Most of all, I love knowing that I am a child of the King and I am covered by the blood of Jesus. He is my Deliver, my Healer, my Rock, my Best Friend, my Counselor, my Burden Bearer, the Voice of Reason, and He cares about every little detail that touches my life. I can rest in Him, trust in Him, and find HOPE in Him, believing His promises to carry me through.

You see, it's one thing to praise God when everything is going well, the bills are paid, the kids think you are a cool mom, the scales are registering at your desired weight, the hubby is giving you tender kisses, and everything seems hunky-dory. But it's another thing to praise God when you are right smack dab in the middle of a whirlwind of drama, under spiritual attack, or walking through a crisis. You let the enemy see you praising God in spite of your circumstance, and that ole devil is gonna be nervous! One of our most powerful warfare weapons is PRAISE! Praise will takes the focus off of ourselves and our problem and help us focus on the POWER of God.

DO YOU LONG FOR CHANGE?

GET A G.R.I.P.

In what area are you struggling right now? Are you stressed out, burned out, and about to pull your hair out? Are you feeling overwhelmed, confused, unheard, unworthy, and filled with worry? If you need a change, it's time to get a G.R.I.P.

**Now may the God of hope fill you with all joy and peace in believing, that you may abound in hope by the power of the Holy Spirit. Romans 15:13 (NKJV)**

# Part II

# Devotional Nuggets

# Can God Forgive My Broken Past?

**H**er voice began to break, and the tears flowed swiftly down the side of her face. I placed her trembling hands within mine and began to squeeze them tightly. I could sense the pain, anguish, and shame as she began to fearfully share with me how she had chosen to end her pregnancy by aborting her child. *"I feel so ugly, so sinful. I took my child's life and it was all because I wanted an easy way out. I was so selfish. How can God ever forgive* me?*"*

She then went on to describe to me how she had awakened from the procedure at that stale, cold abortion clinic and felt so all alone. Her story was filled with so much pain as she spoke about the remorse and sadness she felt. I found myself as her counselor growing bitter, frustrated, and teary eyed as she recounted the harsh, apathetic tone in the nurse's voice, whose only advice had been, *"Here take this heat pad and sit in that chair until you get yourself together. Everything will be just fine..."*

Yet, everything had not been just fine. This young mother had been haunted by her hidden, past sin; awakened many nights to the false cries of a baby; attacked by lies from the enemy that she was worthless, would never measure up, and how God could never forgive her broken past. For years, the sorrow and guilt from this unmentionable secret had weighed heavy upon her, until all the joy had been sapped from her young life.

**God Offers Restoration**

I found myself sitting in that office chair thinking back to some of the decisions I had made in my past. Sinful decisions and poor judgment that at one time in my life wounded friendships, almost destroyed my marriage, grieved my family, and nearly cost me everything. Regrets that for so long caused a deep constant pain and overwhelming shame.

You see the fact is, **we are all just one poor decision away from changing the rest of our lives.** There are times that the enemy will come at you like a howling wolf, with sharp fangs, just foaming at the mouth with his one intention–to attack your mind, create confusion, scar your memories with shame, and make you believe that you cannot break free from the dreaded bondage of your past.

The truth is we cannot break free from our sin on our own, but in Christ there is healing, freedom, forgiveness, and restoration for you no matter what you have done!

*"I waited patiently for the LORD; he turned to me and heard my cry. He lifted me out of the slimy pit, out of the mud and mire; he set my feet on a rock and gave me a firm place to stand. He put a new song in my mouth, a hymn of praise to our God. Many will see and fear and put their trust in the LORD."* **Psalm 40:1-3 (NIV)**

**Breaking Free From The Guilt of Your Past**

There are some of you reading this right now, and you have been trapped in the guilt of your hidden past sin for so long. You have allowed that scum bag, pathetic, scally-wag Satan to convince you that you can never be forgiven. Adultery, coveting, pornography, addictions, a past abortion, a hidden sexual sin, harsh words, stealing...it is time to remind yourself to rely on the grace of GOD and the **POWER** of the Holy Spirit, and rest in the assurance of knowing that GOD loves you and wants to forgive you. Stop living a defeated life and hanging onto your past. **NOTHING, absolutely NOTHING you have ever done can cause God to love you any more or any less!**

The Word of God tell us that when we repent and confess, that our GOD is FAITHFUL to forgive us. No matter how bad your situation may have been, no matter how much pain or anguish you may have caused someone else, no matter how bitter the words or how hurtful the gossip was that leapt from your tongue, God's love, mercy, and Jesus' death on the cross covers it all.

If you have turned from your sins to follow Jesus, then glory to GOD, those chains have fallen, you have been set free! You have been **FORGIVEN** for what happened days, months, or even years ago!

Hallelujah! I praise my GOD, because I have been forgiven of my past. By his wounds, I am healed. In Christ I am a new creation. So don't judge me, Beverly Weeks, by my past, because I no longer reside there!

*"Therefore, there is now no condemnation for those who are in Christ Jesus, because through Christ Jesus the law of the Spirit who gives life has set you free from the law of sin and death."* **Romans 8:1-2 (NIV)**

# Breaking Free From Insecurities

*T*he applause left me speechless. The crowd was cheering so loud, yet still above all the noise, I could hear his hushed whisper as he leaned into the microphone and spoke the words I had been longing to hear, *"I love you. Will you marry me?"* My head was spinning, my knees felt weak, and my heart beat fiercely out of control. I could not believe that my boyfriend had just asked me to be his wife in an unexpected, whirlwind of a marriage proposal. The college auditorium was filled to capacity and it seemed as if all eyes were resting on me, waiting anxiously for my response. ***"YES, I will marry you!"***

The evening was filled with so much laughter, many well wishes, dreams, and hopes, until I received the call that shattered it all into a million broken pieces. The young woman on the other end of the line proceeded to tell me that she had been sexually intimate with my fiancé only days before, and had been secretly involved in an ongoing relationship with him. I dropped the phone, fell to the floor, and cried out in pain. Everything within me ached. I longed just to close my eyes in hopes of later waking to find out it was all a bad dream...

How? Why? When? The questions seemed to flood my mind and immediately they were overshadowed by haunting insecurities. Was she prettier than me? What color were her eyes? Was she smarter than me? Did she share the same interests that I did with him?

My self-esteem was pounced on–I was humiliated, bitter, mortified, and right then and there in that very dark moment, I gave in to every one of those insecurities and chose to believe that I would never measure up...

I allowed that low self-esteem to take up deep roots in my mind, and just like the enemy had planned all along, I found myself caught up in the bondage of a pitiful cycle of foolishness, low self-worth, and sinful coveting. I sunk deeper and deeper into the pit of people pleasing and destructive, toxic dating relationship patterns.

Even many years later after marrying my husband, I catered to those lingering insecurities that blurred my vision. I allowed them to enter my marriage and our bedroom. Those past hurts and deception from that ex-boyfriend, caused me to cringe at the slightest thought of getting naked or transparent before my husband.

That pain from the past broken relationship was excruciating. It left me fearful, always anticipating the worst. It was not until years ago when GOD restored my marriage and fully redeemed our home that I was able to say, ENOUGH IS ENOUGH! **I REFUSE to live like this any longer.** Do you know that change doesn't always come overnight? I had to turn it all over to GOD, be ready to learn, grow, and to heal. In order to break free from this bondage, some things had to take place.

**FORGIVE –** You see, perhaps you don't feel beautiful because of something that has been said or done to you in your past. **Did you know that forgiveness is not optional**? I had to forgive that young lady and that man from my past from all the pain, hurt, and wrong they caused me. You might be struggling as you read this because you need to forgive some hurtful words that have been spoken to you, or some gossip that has been shared about you by someone in your past, a family member, a friend, or even a co-worker. You need to let it go and let GOD be the soothing salve that heals your wounds.

**PRAY**– I don't want to sugar coat this for you. There have been mornings when I have just laid awake in my bed and prayed: *GOD, I need You to take control of my thoughts, ease my broken heart, fill my voids, and help me to be grateful for the way that You have so intricately formed every little thing about me, from my eyes, to my arms, to my corny sense of humor. I praise You, Father, for I am fearfully and wonderfully made.* In my prayer time, I have had to come against those attacks of low self-worth in the name of Jesus!

**TRANSFORM YOUR MIND-** In Romans 12:2 (NIV), the Bible says**,** *Do not conform to the pattern of this world,* ***but be transformed by the renewing of your mind.*** *Then you will be able to test and approve what God's* ***will is****—his good, pleasing and perfect will.*

Notice something with me. That verse does NOT read, *be transformed on an annual basis, on a Sunday morning, once a month, every two years, only when you are feeling low basis.* I am confident God is saying, *be transformed by the renewing of your mind on a daily, even minute by minute basis.* Do you think for one moment that those thoughts I had allowed myself to dwell on were the will of GOD? Good? Pleasing? Perfect? Have mercy, NO, they were not!

Honeychild, I ain't gonna lie! **Yes**, **yes, YES,** there are days that I look in the mirror and the enemy comes at me and says, *who are you fooling, you will never* *measure up! Just give in and give up.*

Yet, in that moment, my spitfire, drama mama, spunkified, not going down without a fight personality comes forth, and I have been known to yell out to the top of my lungs, and rattle the shingles off of my roof: **SHUT UP SATAN,** *you, your LIES, these insecurities and deception can go right straight back to the pits of hell! You no longer have a hold on me. I am beautiful, I am the apple of my Father's eye, I am royalty, I am qualified, I am LOVED, valued, and desired, and above all forever more, I AM and will always be a child of the Most High KING!*

# We Prepared for This, and This, but not THAT!

*I* had not seen that look of distraught on his face since the day he stood beside the gravesite of his brother who'd been unexpectedly taken away at such a young age. I glanced his way and proceeded to vacuum the floor, all the while ignoring my husband's question. Each time my sinful, self-seeking desires had drawn my thoughts away from my commitment to my spouse and had left me blind-sided to the false hopes of finding affirmation and happiness from another man.

## The Adulterous Heart

My cheating on my spouse never involved sex, touching, or even the slightest kiss. It didn't have to. I had already committed adultery in my heart. It began with innocent texts, emails, phone calls, and running into each other at the same restaurant. At first, I tried to justify the relationship by saying that he was just a "friend." He was so easy to talk to, we could openly discuss the frustrations in both of our marriages, and he seemed to understand what I was going through. The secret conversations were followed by months of numerous deleted text messages. It soon led to my coveting and desiring "the greener grass" that other married couples had. My ungodly fantasies led me to seeking a way out of my marriage.

## We Prepared For This, and This, But Not THAT

Didn't I deserve to be happy? I mean, isn't that what

marriage is all about, *my* happiness? For years, my husband and I had been caught up in the **affair of 'things.'** We had gotten our priorities so out of line. We had anxiously prepared for kids, college, retirement, living debt free, that we devoted all of our time to careers, PTA, civic groups, kids' activities, and church "stuff" that we had no energy left to invest in our marriage.

If this makes any sense, we had gotten to the place where we were merely living together as roommates. We had prepared for this, this, and this, but not **THAT!** I am reminded of the story of a spiritual attack on Job in the Bible. In Job 3:25, Job said, *"**That** which I feared has come upon me."* You see, Job had prepared for everything. He was wealthy, influential, had great things and a large family, but he had not anticipated the **'that'** which attacked his family.

**S.O.S. Tips for Moving Forward After an Affair**

When there is admission or discovery of an affair, everything begins to spin out of control. At times your world will seem like it is falling apart and crashing down around you. But you can move forward and begin to make God honoring decisions that are in the best interest of you, your spouse, your marriage, and your family.

**"For nothing is impossible with God." Luke 1:37 (NIV)**

The word *nothing* in this scripture tells me that even your broken marriage can be completely restored. We serve a powerful God!

**Stop and Take Control of Your Thoughts** - The enemy will jolt and attack your mind with the what ifs, whys, the how could you, the blaming, the doubting, bitterness, anger, hurt, and more. You will have to take control of your thoughts. Infidelity is a very difficult and painful situation. Can I just get real with you? For us, as a couple, it involved all kinds of emotions. In all honesty, even as a Christian, you might find it stretching your faith almost to the breaking point. The best thing to do is to **"Turn all your worries over to Him. He cares about you,"** from 1 Peter 5:7. Determine to let God be your Comforter and allow Him to provide you with wisdom and direction on a daily basis.

**Obey to God** – For the healing to take place, my husband and I had to be willing to pray together, to hear one another's hearts, and to offer forgiveness to one another. We cried, we read lots of godly resources, we cried even more, and for the first time we realized that for the change to come to our marriage, it had to begin within our own hearts.

Even though it was painful, I had to accept the responsibility for my actions and the gravity of what I had done to my family. My first step towards reconciliation was to fall on my knees and repent to my God and then to seek forgiveness from my husband.

**Surround Yourself With Godly Counsel** – Is the advice being whispered in your ear godly Biblical advice? If not, you need to **RUN** from it as fast as you can. When we hit this crisis in our marriage, there were all kinds of people wanting to offer advice. People who hardly even knew us; people who had been unsuccessful in honoring their own marriage covenants.

Ask yourself, *"Does this advice fit the character and nature of God as portrayed in the Bible?"* In every area of our lives, we should always test to see whether the counsel we receive is true and honest, just, pure, loving, of good report and would glorify God.

## It's Okay To Reach Out For Help

I'm not going to candy coat this for you. There were hurt, bruised feelings and some pride issues that we had to lay down. Satan loves to intimidate and isolate. My husband and I realized that it was okay to reach out for help, and we recognized that in order for healing and restoration to continue we needed sound, biblical, Christian marriage counseling.

*"Where no counsel is, the people fall: but in the multitude of counselors there is safety."* **Proverbs 11:14 (KJV)**

I am in awe of how GOD has redeemed our marriage. Years later, I can say our marriage is better than it has ever been. We have an emotional intimacy like never before. I love him more today than I did the day we were married.

Are you finding yourself in the fight of your life, struggling just to keep your marriage together? Whatever you may be facing, turn to Him as you face it, because nothing, **ABSOLUTELY NOTHING** is impossible with God!

# Even Noah Looked Foolish!

**W**ARNING: What you are about to read is a true story. The names have not been changed to protect the foolish, um, I mean innocent. It was another one of those can it, could it, would it, yes it can, it could, it would, and it DID happen to sweet, little, innocent ol' me moments in my life.

The passion was slowly disintegrating in my marriage, and I knew without a doubt that this wife needed to implement some swift changes in the romance department where my marriage was concerned. I'll admit, I had somewhat been a teeny, tiny bit, unknowingly deficient in the area of expressing my feelings and flirting with my hubby, Rick.

Shucks fire, in my past I had hardly ever been the type of wife to send her husband a text or drop an email once an hour, or even on a daily basis just to say, "Hey, I love you," or to encourage him. Isn't it amazing that we, as women, want to be pursued, and we crave romance from our husbands, yet we often forget that they desire the same thing?

## Foolish in Love: Oh, no she didn't!

Nervously, I pulled out my cell phone and sent my husband Rick the following text: *"You R a hunk! Thinking of u & I can't wait 2 snuggle & get a hold of your luscious lips! I got a prize waiting for u when u get home!:) Love, Bev"*

Within minutes, I began to fidget at my desk waiting eagerly for his response. I knew my text would blow my hubby's mind. I just prayed it wouldn't give him a severe life altering heart attack! The clock ticked, minutes passed, and it seemed like hours. Finally, I heard the "DING" sound indicating an incoming message. I scuffled to pick up my cell phone, which displayed the following reply: *"Dear Bev, I am sure you intended to send this message to your husband & not to me, although I did get excited!"*

**Have Mercy Sista!**

Grab the peanut butter and chocolate, this is the part where the story gets water cooler, bellyaching, giggling good! At that very moment, I dropped the phone and screamed out, *"Lord, help me!!!"*

I had inadvertently sent that steamy message to the last person I dialed that morning. He was a contractor and business acquaintance who I called that morning to request his consideration in signing a proposal I had submitted to his company.

My office buddies gathered around my desk and laughed and joked about it for days. Afterwards, every time I spoke with that contractor, he would chuckle. Needless to say, I NEVER have forgotten that incident.

**Looking Foolish: To Be Sure I'm NOT the Only One**

Have you ever done something FOOLISH? I mean down right, tee-totally embarrassing, let me cover my face, or crawl into a hole nearby, foolish? I am reminded there will be days in my Christian walk with God, when I take a stand for my Lord, that I may appear to look absurd, nutty, or plain ol' foolish to some people. You may be feeling that way even now as you take a stand for your own marriage.

Your friends may be saying *"Are you crazy? Drop him!"* But yet, you continue to STAND on the Word of God and claim His promises. Maybe you are looking foolish because you have been praying day and night for a breakthrough in your finances, your job, a relationship with someone in your family, a prodigal child, or a friend at your church. All the while, the people you admire most are laughing at you.

### Even Noah Looked Foolish

Can you imagine just how foolish Noah and his sons appeared to look when God told Noah to build the ark? That boat was 450 feet long (the length of 1.5 football fields) 75 feet wide and 45 feet high, about the height of a five-story building. I am sure his neighbors and closest friends gathered around and they laughed their heads off. *"Hey Noah, are you crazy!? There ain't but so many trout over there in that water. You are a foolish man building a boat this big! Oh, and Noah, how do you expect to drag it to the water?"*

But Noah was obedient to God. He began to share how there was going to be a great flood and how they needed to repent. Let me tell you, I bet there was a whole lot of gossiping and giggling until those first water-filled, dark, stormy clouds rolled in!

**There will be times when we as Christians look foolish. BUT most of those times will be because we are doing God's will and doing God's work.**

I want to be a risk taker. I, Beverly Weeks, want to seize opportunities, embrace uncertainty, and with my dragon slaying spiritual weapons in hand, I want to face my deepest, darkest fears and insecurities head on. I want to be all that GOD has created me to be, and absolutely nothing less.

For too long, I have allowed the enemy to stifle my God-given potential. I have been guilty in my past of entertaining that voice in my mind that says, *you're not qualified, this will never work;* that pesky voice of doubt that says, *are you sure you have been called.* **Not any longer!**

**I am committed. I am resolved. I am going forth in VICTORY.** I am taking a stand for my Jesus. Just like Noah, I will dare to look foolish!

*"Take delight in the LORD, and he will give you the desires of your heart."* **Psalm 37:4 (NIV)**

# Facing an Unexpected Storm

*I* sat on the end of my bed, holding my hands over my face, and began to weep uncontrollably. I felt so alone, torn, confused, ashamed, and bitter. Because of my poor choices and sinful, selfish desires, my entire world had come crashing down. My marriage was falling apart right before my eyes, and I did not even recognize the phony person I had become. My thoughts were being haunted by the images of fear and anxiety that overshadowed my two small children's faces. ***How had I allowed myself to have feelings for another man?***

I had been involved in church all of my life--taught Sunday school, participated in church programs, the choir–and now I found myself right smack dab in the middle of a violent unexpected spiritual storm. Just like an out of control tornado, this storm had erupted, swept in, and caught my family completely off guard. It seemed as if the turbulent, high-speed winds and waves were caving in all around me. They threatened to bring me down.

## The Despair of the Storm

My heart was filled with so much discouragement. The enemy had me just where he wanted me. I felt as if there was no hope. How would "we" ever get out of this tangled mess? How could "I" fix something so broken? How could my husband and family ever trust me again? How could I ever allow myself to forgive my enemies for their bitter words? How would I ever repair the financial hardship and strain I placed on our family by forcing my husband to live away from the home we had come to love? That storm caused so much damage and despair.

## I Couldn't Fix a Thing

I couldn't fix a thing! I needed a healer, a restorer, a rebuilder, a comforter, an encourager, a close friend. Broken, humbled, and desperate for answers, I looked toward the ceiling of my bedroom and cried out to GOD with everything that was in me. *GOD, I need you to come to my rescue! Everything looks hopeless.* It was in the arms of my loving Savior that I found **REFUGE.**

**"God is our refuge and strength, a very present help in trouble. Therefore will not we fear, though the earth be removed, and though the mountains be carried into the midst of the sea; though the waters thereof roar and be troubled, though the mountains shake with the swelling thereof. Selah."Psalm 46:1-3. (KJV)**

**R: Redeemer/Restorer-** Only God can put the pieces back together again. Whatever the enemy has tried to take away from you, GOD wants to restore it. Fix your eyes on Jesus, the Author and Perfector of our faith! Take back what belongs to you. Today I am declaring no more wasted time and, no more stolen years, relationships, finances, or health in my life. God will restore and rebuild the broken areas in your life. Through His restoration power, NOTHING is wasted.

**E: Enough-** GOD is more than enough. For so long, I had depended on other people to fill all my needs. I was expecting my husband to be my God. I was so wrong. I discovered there is only One who can satisfy. You see, regardless of what is going on all around you, our GOD is still on His throne! The resources of heaven have NOT been depleted. Right now, you may be in a panic filled state of mind in the middle of this storm, but GOD is not the slightest bit worried. He saw this coming long before you did. He is still large and very much in charge!

**F: Faithful** – There were so many things that I had placed my trust in: comfortable savings account, a beautiful two story home, a nice car, friends, clothes, and my job. I learned that there is only one unfailing, unchanging thing, and that is my GOD's faithfulness. We can follow, believe, trust, and be comforted in the fact that the GOD we serve is faithful to all that love him, faithful even to the very end. He is loyal, He is constant, and He is steadfast. He does not abandon us. Friends and family members may desert us, but our **GOD will always be faithful!**

*"Know therefore that the LORD your God is God; he is the faithful God, keeping his covenant of love to a thousand generations of those who love him and keep his commandments."* **Deuteronomy 7:9 (NIV)**

**U: Unparalleled-** There is none like Him! No one compares to God Almighty. He is unequalled and unparalleled in His greatness, His kindness, and His love.

**G: God Almighty-** In Genesis 17:1 and Genesis 35:11, He says, *"I am the Almighty God."*

My God can do and undo. He can open doors that no man can shut, and shuts doors that no man can open. He can create divine opportunities, restore checking and savings accounts, redeem broken marriages, and heal disease even when the doctors have lost all hope. My God can breathe life into your hopeless situation. **He is ALMIGHTY!**

**E: Everlasting** - Our God is an everlasting God. He has been here since before the beginning of creation; He will continue to be there even when the world has passed away. There is but ONE God.

**GOD IS MY REFUGE!**

Storms will come. We will face tragedies and unexpected warfare. I don't care how anointed or how spiritual you are, there is an enemy and he is on a desperate mission. The Bible says he has come to **kill, steal, and destroy**! Buckle down; get ready for the strong winds, the lightning, and thunder. Be prayed up, in the Word of God and remember GOD IS WITH YOU in the midst of the storm. *He wants to be your REFUGE.*

# The "I Want It Now!" Syndrome

*J*ust being candid, it is undeniably one of my worst faults. It surpasses my gluttonous desire for white chocolate covered Oreos, red velvet cake, dark chocolate, peanut butter, creamy Alfredo sauce, and anything deep-fried. It's what I call the terrible, frustrating, mind boggling, bondage holding, epidemic of the *I WANT IT NOW* syndrome!

*Lord, I have got to lose this weight NOW. You know I've got a speaking engagement on Friday, so if You can help me lose ten pounds by 5:30 p.m. so I can fit "that" dress, and while You're at it, can You give me a raise by the end of the week so I can buy new shoes, and heal this cough by Wednesday, change my husband by Thursday...and I want it NOW!*

Anybody know what I'm talking about? *Lord, You have got to mend this relationship NOW, I need this job NOW, You need to bless our finances NOW, change my kids' hearts now, take away this pain NOW, open this ministry door NOW...*

## It Didn't Just Come On Me Overnight

I confess that I had this syndrome way before adulthood. As a freckled-faced, snaggle-tooth preschooler, I was known to throw a couple of daring, *'let me test my momma'* tantrums to get my way in the grocery store. I wanted that toy, candy, or miniature lip gloss at the check-out line, and I would do anything to get it NOW! I have fallen to the floor, kicked, screamed, held my breath, turned blue, and I have even been known to throw in a little fake foaming at the mouth just to get what I want.

I could have stolen that soap opera Emmy Award from Young & The Restless many times! BUT... Well, speaking of "buts," when my momma got a hold of my butt... well, glory!! That is a *'hole 'notha* story...

## Be Careful What You Ask For NOW!

Years followed, and I became old enough to date. I honestly can remember praying: *Lord, please let me date 'him' now.* And then there was 'him,' and 'him,' and 'him.' *Lord, if you love me, let 'him' ask me out now!! Hurry Lord, don't You want me to be happy? You don't want me to be single all my life, do You?"*

Just the other day, I ran into one of the *'hims'* I had desperately begged, prayed and asked God to allow me to date. He was sitting in a restaurant eating his fourth burger, mustard all over his face, using vulgar language...can I just say... *Glory! Hallelujah! Thank You, Lord, for not answering that prayer when I wanted it NOW!!*

## God's "NO" Was Not Rejection, but REDIRECTION

For so long I was guilty of trying to rush God's will for my life. Many times what I wanted "**NOW**" is not what I truly needed. There were times looking back that God was saying *'not quite yet, I am still working and refining some things so that when I give it to you, it will blow your mind!'*

You see I am learning that God knows when saying 'yes' could possibly bring me harm that I didn't foresee, or He may be saying, *I need you to wait while*

59

*I am cultivating some much needed patience and persistence in you to build your faith even greater...*

**Let Go and Let GOD!**

I have learned humbly to let go, and let God take control. **I will admit, it has not always been easy.** There have been nights that I have cried out to God and felt like those prayers were ricocheting back from the bedroom ceiling. I will tell you though, that never once has my God failed me.

Although I don't always understand or cannot fathom why He would not answer the way I want, God knows what is best for me. He cares about every little detail and concern that touches my life. You see, often times our focus is on the instant, getting it NOW, all the while God's focus is eternity. He sees the big picture. Waiting teaches us to trust God. God's will is worth the wait and I want to be right smack dab in the middle of it!

***"Show me your ways, Lord, teach me your paths. Guide me in your truth and teach me, for you are God my Savior, and my hope is in you all day long."* Psalm 25:4-5 (NIV)**

# Forgiving Harsh Words

*"You make me sick, you will never ever amount to anything, you are such a loser! How dare you walk away from your marriage."*

My lips quivered and my eyes swelled with tears as I read the condemning email I had received. What made it even more hurtful and unbearable was that the words were from a friend, someone who I truly loved and respected.

I could not believe the spiteful verbal assault being lashed out at me. Fear, anger, and bitterness began to consume me. My emotions were in such turmoil. As I glanced in the car mirror at my swollen eyes, and flushed red cheeks, the words replayed in my mind over and over again. They choked out any positive thought I had of my husband and I restoring our shattered marriage. I felt completely abandoned and alone and began to have a total meltdown.

The sharp, biting words came at a time when my husband and I were secretly struggling in our marriage. I will not deny that some of the accusations hurled my way were partly true.

Involved emotionally with a close male friend and under strong conviction, I already felt I was being attacked in every area of my life. For months, even after reconciliation with my husband, I would pull those words from the email I had printed and rehash them. I allowed the message to take control over my crushed, low self-esteem. I chose to hold onto the hurts and I was miserable.

***I sense in my spirit that some of you may also have been the victim of harsh words.*** Maybe they were shared by a friend, a family member, a co-worker, or even your spouse.

I can think of several occasions when my husband and I were tired, frustrated, overcommitted, dealing with uncertainty, under a financial burden, and we didn't think before we spoke. Instead we lashed out at each other.

You know that is a numbing, raw kind of pain. You hold on tight to those words and harbor feelings of resentment. I have even been guilty of the *word war game.* You may know what I mean...*if he is going to throw harsh words my way, I will make him pay deeply!* So I don't speak to him for days. I ignore him, or even withhold sex as a punishment. In the end, no one wins, the problem is not resolved, and it leads to even deeper hurt.

***My friend, not only is unforgiveness a sin, but it will eat at you to the core, and eventually destroy you like a growing cancer that consumes a life.*** I read that medical science has linked a failure to forgive with all kinds of ailments, including stress, anxiety, depression, headaches, back aches, stomach distress, diabetes, hypertension, and heart problems. While granting forgiveness isn't easy, **it is also not optional** - our Lord commands it in Matthew 6:14 as a prerequisite for our own sins being forgiven.

**Forgiveness can't be based on a feeling. You have to make the choice to forgive.** I will not lie, there have been times that the pain was so haunting, and I just did not "feel" like forgiving. Often times my pain did not subside until I made that choice. You may be thinking, *but I was wronged, I was hurt, how will I ever forget what they did to me?* Truth is, you may never fully forget. If someone hurt one of my children or did something harmful to one of my family members, you bet your bottom dollar it would be hard to forget!

**Granting forgiveness is not saying you are letting this person off the hook**. Instead, it is saying, *I choose to obey God. I can't handle this anymore by myself, I can't solve this. This hurts too much. Father GOD, I am placing this situation in Your hands and I am trusting You to take care of it.*

When you forgive, you are letting go. You will no longer allow this incident to control your thoughts, change you, or hurt you any longer. In addition, you are giving up your right to hurt that person back. You release this hurt and vengeance to God.

**Do you need to forgive someone? Maybe you need to seek someone's forgiveness? Ask God to lead you today to release it to Him.**

*"...forgiving each other, just as in Christ God forgave you."* **Ephesians 4:32 (NIV)**

# God, Help Me I'm Scared!

*T*he pain swooped fiercely through my head. I could hardly stand the throbbing in my temples. My vision grew blurry, and from out of nowhere, the severe headache caught me by surprise. In less than an hour, I had gone from laughter and my usual fun, outgoing, quirky self to being knocked flat off my size eight feet with a paralyzing, nauseating migraine.

I found myself lying on the sofa in the pitch dark, crying out to God for some sort of instant relief. Immediately my mind filled with panic, what ifs, anxiety, farfetched thoughts, and assumptions that had me in an uproar as to what my medical diagnosis could possibly be.

You see I'm good at preaching to others about not worrying, but at that moment in a crippling physical situation, I tee-totally flipped out! My first response was completely opposite of what I had always shared. I grew anxious and panicked.

## God, I'm Filled With Fear

I think back to a time when my marriage began to crumble. I was walking around living a lie, acting as if I had it all together, yet deep inside I was lonely. I was craving a distorted life of excitement, and tangled up in an emotional affair which had me spiraling out of control and plunging down into a pit of coveting, discontentment, secrets, and hidden sin.

64

My hurtful, selfish actions caused my husband to sink into depression. My children were filled with grief, fear, and so confused that they walked around our home like little zombies.

## God, I'm So Broken & Confused

Some of you know all too well what panic feels like. Perhaps you found yourself in the middle of a broken marriage or relationship. It could be that you're going through a devastating separation period, or walking through a messy divorce. Maybe it's your finances, a situation with a prodigal child, attacks of gossip, worries with your job, or circumstance with your health, and just like me, you want to cry out, **God, help me I'm scared!**

## The Enemy is a LIAR!!

Listen my friend, I don't care how good a person you are, how gifted, anointed, or spiritual you are. You can teach Sunday School, sing in the choir, or even be the lead pastor; the attacks will come! The enemy will haunt your mind with thoughts of fear and doubt, and convince you that things will never get better, you will always be stuck in a rut, you don't deserve any better, you are getting just what you deserve, this is all your fault, and there is no such thing as forgiveness, healing, or restoration.

I want you to know that Satan is a liar!!! In the name of Jesus, you need to grab that imaginary two by four and go to swinging with all the power that GOD has given you and slam that scally-wag, backstabbing, betraying, defaming, falsifying rascal and all his pathetic little demons in the head!! Things may look grim and have you down. Your mind may be swirling in a furious tizzy, haunted with questions, but OUR

GOD has promised we WILL overcome! We don't have to reside and take up residence in the pit of panic.

There is rest for the weary and there is hope for the faint at heart. There is a ridiculous, life altering PEACE that can come to us as Christians when we began to pray, get in the word of GOD, call upon and cry out the mighty name of Jesus. My friend, you can rest in the promise of knowing that GOD saw this situation coming long before you did, and He has it under control!

God breathed life into my dead marriage. I have seen Him as I stood by the graveside and watched my mother-in-law bury her 33 year old son. I have seen Him as I sat in the doctor's office and received the news that I had a lump. I have seen Him restore broken finances. I KNOW, without a doubt, that my GOD is still in the miracle making, mind-boggling, life changing restoration business. What are you needing God to do for you today?

# God, Are You Even Listening?

*I* hit my fist on the desk and shook my head in despair. Why God? You know I have deadlines, a speaking engagement to prepare for, and on top of that, I've exhausted all my resources and I am running out of time. I looked up to the ceiling in my office as if God was standing right over me, and then I wept as I blurted out, ***God are you even listening?***

Only hours before, a young mother had walked into the crisis pregnancy center where I worked, seeking information on terminating her pregnancy. She found herself alone with a young son, no money, entangled in a past addiction to pain killers, and feeling like no one could possibly care.

I looked her in the eyes and began to share with her that God cares about her and loves her no matter what she could have possibly ever done. Through her bitter tears, she spoke of how poor choices had led her to little money and nowhere for her and her eight-year-old son to stay. For the first time in her life, she was homeless–evicted with no place to go.

After sharing the gospel with her and giving her all her pregnancy options, this beautiful, broken, mother decided to give her unborn child life. Yet, I knew in order to show this mother the true love of Christ, I had to do more than just talk the talk. I needed to find her a temporary place to stay and get her, the unborn child, and her young son off the street.

## When You've Done All You Can Do

I contacted every homeless shelter, exhausted every community lead, and because of an already strained ministry budget, there was no extra funding for a hotel room.

I found myself staring at a blank computer screen, and through my tears I began to pray. *God I need a word from You. Lord, I need to show this young mother that I care. She has chosen to give her unborn child life and I want to help her, but I have done everything I possibly can.*

## Desperate To Hear From God

Have you ever been there? When you just wanted to fall to your knees and cry out, *God can You even hear me? Don't You care? God, are You listening?*

Maybe you're in a similar situation now. Maybe your marriage is falling apart. He has walked out. You've read the books, bought him gifts, wrote letters, cried, shared your feelings, and it seems absolutely NOTHING you are doing is working.

It could be your finances. You've paid your tithes, you've given up things that you really wanted, and it still seems that you can't make the ends meet. Perhaps it's the emotional exhaustion from dealing with a prodigal child, attacks of gossip, a bad situation at work, an unexpected doctor's report, failed attempts to get healthy, or the stress and strain of life. You want to scream out just like I did, *GOD, are You even listening?*

## F.A.I.T.H.: For All I Trust Him!

I find myself weeping and rejoicing each time I share

the rest of my client's story. I will never forget the
knock on my door that afternoon. The godly ladies
stood there and explained how the Lord had led them
to our center at the very time I had been praying and
banging my fist on that desk. I get chills just thinking
about it!

We stood there in that foyer, held hands together. We
cried and thanked God for his goodness. Afterwards,
those dear precious ladies, total strangers, wrote out
personal checks to provide my client a hotel room.
God had heard my cry.

**Without a doubt, we can put our trust in the
fact that the God we serve does not lie. He never
changes, and His Word stands true forever**. There
have been times when this ol' girl has been fearful and
disillusioned, searching for God and wondering *are
You there Lord? I can't see or feel a thing happening in
my situation.*

BUT, I have come to know that no matter what I
see through these earthly eyes, no matter how grim
things appear, even when I am numb and can't feel a
thing, through every difficulty, every storm, when it
seems all hell is breaking loose, **MY GOD IS THERE!**
He is working and moving in my situation, refining
me, using every little detail that the enemy meant to
harm me with and turning it around for my good and
for His glory.

*"A hostile world! I call to God, I cry to God to
help me. From his palace he hears my call; my
cry brings me right into his presence— a private
audience!"* **Psalm 18:6 The Message (MSG)**

I have learned that my difficulties have tremendous
power to change me for better or worse. I can choose

to be bitter, or I can choose to say, *God I am going to depend on You and have the FAITH that You are gonna see me through.*

In what area are you needing some miraculous, shifting to take place?

I want you to pray this with me:

**Lord, I am in the middle of desperate situation. I hurt, I ache, I am broken, and I need You. Father, I am going to hold on and wait for You to show me Your love and goodness no matter what happens. God, I am trusting in You. I ask for wisdom and clarity in my circumstance. In the name of Jesus I pray, Amen.**

# He Walked Out, Insecurities Walked In

*I* could feel my knees collapsing as I helplessly fell to the floor weeping. I began to gasp for breath. The anxiety, bitterness, and depression began to attack and hover over me like a mad cluster of swarming killer bees.

My mind and thoughts were invaded by questions. *What did she look like? Was she prettier than me? Was she skinnier than me? What color hair did she have, was it long, was it wavy? Did she dress better than me, did she make him laugh the way I did?* The room felt as if it were spinning out control and as I sat there alone and broken, the resentment began to take over.

**I thought we were supposed to spend the rest of our lives together. How could this be happening?** I was in my twenties and he was the first man I had fallen in love with. Only hours before, he had asked me to be his wife on stage in front of a packed college auditorium. Now I had received this devastating call from a woman from his past claiming to be involved in an intimate ongoing relationship with him. How could I have not known? **I felt so ugly, so victimized, and so worthless.** There was the confrontation, the tears, the attempts at reconciliation, but later it all crumbled and he just walked away.

Even though this relationship happened years before I met my husband, the memory still lingered. Just being candid, for so long I was guilty of allowing it to cripple me, wreck my securities, and shake my self-worth to the core.

The truth is that some of you reading this right now do not feel beautiful, and you are battling with insecurities and low self-esteem because of what's been done to you in your past. He walked out on you, left you, told you he never loved you, or left you for someone else. Maybe it was a painful divorce and you feel like damaged goods. Maybe it was another broken relationship or even the pain from your own father walking out of your life. **I sense in my spirit even as I am writing this, the hurt and grief is so deep that you just want to walk away and stop reading this.**

Maybe you carry the guilt of being raped or molested. No one knows this hidden secret, or the guilt and the shame associated with it. You try to keep it together, but you replay the absolute hell in your mind over and over again. You begin to ask questions—*was it my fault?* If you don't feel beautiful because any of this happened, let me just stop and remind you—**IT WAS NOT YOUR FAULT.**

Some of you reading this feel ashamed and worthless because of an immoral past. Satan has been attacking and manipulating your mind to where you just feel there is no way you can ever feel beautiful.

Today is your day of **VICTORY! In Christ, we can move from being a victim to walking with Him in victory in our future.** Just being honest, **YES,** in my past I tried counselors. I tried exercising and starving myself for the wrong reasons.

I have tried cracker diets and fad diets, I have worn the provocative fashions, I have stood in front of the mirror weeping uncontrollably, and years ago I even attempted to put my finger down my throat on multiple occasions. Absolutely none of this could take away my pain or make me feel beautiful.

Friend, the change came when I decided to cry out to GOD and say, *I can't take it anymore! I repent. For some reason I have bought the LIE that I am not good enough. I no longer want to hurt. Lord–open my eyes to see how the enemy deceived me in the past. I need YOU, GOD, to make me brand new. I need to be **free** from this bondage. God, help me to get rid of my old self and allow You to begin a work in me. God, help me to love her: the lady in the mirror. Lord, I need healing in my mind and with these damaging memories. I am giving every area of my heart, mind, soul, spirit, and habits to my Lord. **I refuse to be a victim, I claim my VICTORY!** In Jesus' precious name I accept my healing.*

**"You were taught, with regard to your former way of life, to put off your old self, which is being corrupted by its deceitful desires; to be made new in the attitude of your minds; and to put on the new self, created to be like God in true righteousness and holiness." Ephesians 4:22-24 (NIV)**

*If you have experienced sexual abuse, rape or trauma, we strongly encourage you to seek a local Christian counselor and/or trusted pastor to walk with you on the journey of healing. We also encourage you to pray and share it with your spouse; he likely already knows there is something not quite right.*

# How to Change Your Spouse

**N**ervously, I began to fidget, play around with my jewelry, and crack my knuckles as I sat on the brown sofa. It had taken all my courage just to muster up enough strength to walk into the Christian marriage counselor's office.

It just felt so awkward. I mean for years I taught Sunday school, sung in the choir, and now I was having to admit to a total stranger that I did not have it all together. I felt as if my marriage had fallen completely apart. In all honesty, I had already checked out of the marriage relationship. Yet my husband pleaded for me to reach out to her for help.

I went to that counseling session really as a way to appease him. I wanted to be able to tell my friends that I had done everything possible before dissolving the marriage. I guess that deep down, I went secretly hoping that the counselor would affirm my decision to separate from him. At the very least, I had hoped that she could tell me how to change him.

I took a sip from the water bottle, composed myself, and then all of a sudden me and my 160 plus pounds of strong willed A-T-T-I-T-U-D-E decided to blurt out my frustrations: ***"Honey before you say anything, I want you to know that I am not taking him back if HE doesn't change this, this and this..."***

I proceeded to rattle off the things on my list; things

that aggravated me to the core: *"I mean how dare my husband not show me any affection. I feel like he always put his job before me. He never lets me help with making decisions. He is never affectionate. I am a people person and he loves staying at home. I love a clean house and he, well, let's just say we are totally opposite..."*

I began to call them off, one fault right behind the other, until I noticed she wasn't responding or saying very much. Of course, if the truth be known, I didn't give her much of an opportunity! Finally, she lifted her pen, cleared her throat and spoke in a near silent whisper. Her words, which were full of conviction, were not at all what I had wanted to hear. ***"What if God is more interested in changing YOU than in changing your spouse?"***

**I Had To Change Me**

I want you to know that I did not exactly receive her words with the love of Christ! As a matter of fact, my fleshly sinful side wanted to leap off that sofa, pluck every blonde hair out of her head and her eyebrows and shout, *"Lady, seriously, were you not just listening to what I said!?"*

Her words resonated in my ears. For the next few weeks and months, our marriage restoration and healing began with me first recognizing the fact that **I could NOT change my spouse.** No matter how hard I tried, the only person I could change was me. For some time, I had naively thought that if I could just change my husband, it would fix our relationship and the problems would vanish.

**How to Change Your Spouse: The Power of the Two P Words**

75

**PRAY: I began to pray in a new way... Lord, change me.** I remember one night sitting on the end of my bed, staring at the ceiling-weeping and pouring my heart out to God. *"God, You know my heart. You know all the ways my husband has hurt me, all my frustrations, the bitterness and the callous feelings. Lord, You know all my expectations, hopes and my dreams. Father, I realize that I cannot change him so I ask that You will soften my heart; help me to compromise, accept the things that I cannot change, and God use these things that I don't understand to make me stronger. Lord, I give you my marriage. I ask you to untangle the conflicts, strife, and heal my hurts. Help me to see the good in my husband. Renew our love and passion for one another and heal our emotional wounds..."*

Now I won't lie, for weeks it was just plain hard to pray that way. But I noticed over time that things really did begin to change for the better. My reactions changed, my behavior changed, and it triggered my husband to want to make small changes.

**PRAISE: I began to praise my husband.** I learned right quick like that my positive reinforcements to my husband added fuel in his tank. Pretty soon he began to pick up his towels, he began to be more affectionate, and he agreed to go out more. Ironically, every one of the small changes that he had put into place were things I had completely stopped nagging him about. I got rid of these six words from my vocabulary... ***"You have to change or else!"***

You see in the past, my selfish ultimatums had only stirred up bitterness and frustration. I found that my new words–*"Thank you for picking up the towels, thank you for helping in the kitchen, I like it when you hold my hand"*–all of these affirmed him. For the first time in a long time, my husband began to feel respected.

As God began to change my heart, I was able to communicate with my husband more clearly. In the past I would have easily snapped and tore into him. I think my gentle and quiet spirit began to win him over. I am not saying everything was magically fixed. What I am saying is that instead of compressing and stuffing my frustrations (which later almost always led to an explosion,) I began to communicate what I needed from him instead of assuming that he already knew.

**I learned it's not my place to change my husband, that is God's work**. I am not my husband's Holy Spirit! There was lots of compromising, determination, and a whole lot of hard work involved in turning around our marriage. **NO, you cannot change your spouse**, but you can pray that GOD will change you! In return, when GOD softens your heart, your marriage will have no other choice but to change.

# I Just Can't Take it Anymore!

*I* could smell the smoke and charred food and I realized that something just wasn't right. My heart raced as I ran to the kitchen and realized that the oven was on fire.

*Really, God?* Here I am trying to self-clean an oven and the remnants from my old cooking have burst into flames! On top of that, the oven door is locked and I can't even douse the fire with water. *God, do you not see that I am in desperate need of help!?*

Reaching over to get water from the sink, I nearly slipped on a puddle that saturated my floor from the malfunctioned and leaking dishwasher. As if it could not get any worse, I hear a clankety-clank sound from the washing machine, and yes, you guessed it, another major problem!

Three appliances, all needing repairs, and the next paycheck is a week away. I have saved diligently for a new outfit and now that is just not an option. My fourteen year old is yelling, *"I have a game and you have not washed my shorts,"* and then my husband walks through the door, not noticing my state of immense panic, he grabs my hiney, (I know what he is thinking, ughh!) and whispers, *"What's for dinner?"*

At that moment, my fleshly, sinful self wanted to grab him by that suit jacket and shout, *"I just can't take it anymore!"*

May I just get candid and share some truth with you? *"I just can't take it anymore"* is a lie straight from hell and from the devil himself! There have been times in my past that I have chosen not only to listen to that lie, but I allowed it to saturate my mind. I had been guilty of living so far down in the pit of *"woe is me"* that I was comfortable. As a matter of fact, I decided to camp out there for a while.

I got so content in my pit of fears, frustrations and anxiety that, if this makes any sense, I began to hang pictures on the wall, decorate my pit, kick my feet back on my imaginary recliner, grab a jar of peanut butter and a chocolate bar and throw myself a *"pity party"* for one!

To be set free from a lie you have to counter it with the truth. The truth for my situation was that I needed to trust and believe that my GOD'S grace is sufficient for me. His grace is totally sufficient for every critical moment, every crucial circumstance, every need, and every single failure in my life.

When I am exhausted mentally from a long day of chores, from a speaking engagement, or work at the office, and one of my children decides to take a bite out of the other's hamburger for no reason and World War III erupts, and I want to grab them by the seat of the pants and shout, *I can't take it anymore!*

That is when I remind myself, HIS grace is sufficient for me. When I am down to $10 in my checking account on Wednesday, and I realize that neither of us will get paid until Friday, and on Thursday the tire goes flat, the oil light comes on, and the needle is on empty, I can choose to sink into depression or remind myself that HIS grace is sufficient for me!

I remember a time when I was lying in a hospital room as a radiologist began to share an unclear mammogram report. Immediately my mind was filled with fear and questions. On the same day, I left that appointment and went over to the dentist office where I had received a report of a possible cyst forming underneath my gum line. I won't lie, I broke down right there in that dental chair. The first words that came to my mind were *"I just can't take it anymore!"* You know what my Christian dentist shared in so many words with me? God's grace is sufficient!

You might be feeling right now that you just can't go on. Your bills and the mounting debt are so overwhelming, or you may be struggling with your health. Maybe it's a prodigal child that has gone astray, your marriage, a pink slip, pressures of college, and everything just looks hopeless.

Perhaps you are battling with some secret depression, low self-esteem, an addiction, or you look in the mirror and you feel so lost, so all alone and you want to cry out, *I just can't take it anymore!* I want to remind you of these precious words in the Bible, *"My grace is sufficient for you"* in 2 Corinthians 12:9 (NIV).

It's time to stop listening to the enemy. Setting your heart and mind on lies is like setting the radio dial or T.V. channel to a trashy, inappropriate station. What feeds you, will indeed affect you.

*I just can't take it anymore* is a lie! You CAN make it. Surround yourself with godly friends to encourage you. Reach out for help. Read the word of God, run into HIS arms, cry out to God, HIS grace is sufficient for you!

# I Was That Prodigal Wife

*T*he drive on the way home was somber and unusually quiet. There were no sing-alongs, no laughter, no music, only grim silence. It was as if my two young children were mourning and had just left a freshly dug grave. As I turned to reach for his hand, I could see the tears flowing uncontrollably from my young son's eyes. He forcefully pushed my hand away and with his voice breaking, he yelled out, *"I can't take this anymore. Why did we have to leave dad? Mom, what have you become? I want my family back!"*

## What had I become?

For several days his words resonated in my ears. I tried desperately to get the look of his solemn face out of my mind. His face was filled with so much pain, hurt, and so many questions. *Yet, his words were so convicting. What had I become?* My marriage was under attack and my husband and I had drifted apart, but instead of choosing to fight for my marriage, in my discontentment, I selfishly opted for what looked like the easy way out. I had chosen to take the road that I convinced myself would lead to a better life.

## The Prodigal

I found myself living out the life of the parable of the prodigal son. You see, his discontentment had led him straight to a life of coveting and wanting more. Just like that prodigal son, I set out to seek a life of fulfilling my own self-centered pleasures. I can't even imagine the pain and deep anguish the father felt that day when his prodigal son came to him and said, *"Give me what is mine."* In a sense the son was really saying, ***"I wish you were dead! You haven't died soon enough to suit me, I want what is mine now!"***

My hand quivers as I write this next line, I feel my emotions taking over. I have to ponder if years ago when my marriage was broken, did not my husband's heart break in that same way? Oh, how he questioned, how he pleaded, how he cried, when I looked at him and I too said, *"I want out, give me what is mine!"* I wonder if the thought ever once crossed his mind, *does my wife think she'd be better off if I were dead?*

But, just like the father of the prodigal son, my husband prepared his heart, cried out to God, and surrounded himself with godly people to encourage him for my homecoming. Just being candid, I never once had to leave the comfort of our home. It was my husband who was forced to leave. Yet I had chosen to flee from my responsibilities as a wife and a mother.

Months later, after godly intense counsel, repentance, and seeking forgiveness, I was spiritually returning home to my marriage and to my family. I realized the foolishness in my actions and most importantly, I recognized that I was nothing without God. Friends, I was so tired of eating after the swine, tired of flirting with sin, hanging out with people who only liked me for what I could do for them, or for something I was not.

## Celebrate When the Lost Are Found!

But just like the parable of the prodigal son, my story

does not end there. I can hear my husband shouting out to all our neighbors, *get out the fatted calf, turn up the music, let me get her wedding ring cleaned and shined up, I am putting on my finest suit! Kids, put on your best clothes, let's run out to Krispy Kreme and grab her favorite doughnut, stop by the store and load up on her favorite chocolates, God has restored our home! God has redeemed your mother. My beautiful bride is coming home!*

Hallelujah! Are you finding yourself in a desperate situation just like the father of the prodigal son? Or just like my husband with his prodigal wife? Maybe it is a teen-aged son or daughter who walked away? Maybe you are barely holding on as you cry out to God for healing in your marriage and for your prodigal spouse to come home?

Friend, my GOD has sent me to tell you to keep standing, keep praying, meditate on the promises and hope found in the word, surround yourself with godly people who will encourage and lift you up! **As long as you are breathing there is HOPE!** Don't ever give up. Very soon your prodigal may come running home!

***"I pray that the eyes of your heart may be enlightened." Ephesians 1:18 (NIV)***

# L.E.T. G.O. of Bad Habits

**Y**ou've got to be kidding me! There has to be something wrong with this dag-blasted, antiquated bathroom scale. Maybe the battery is low, maybe the bathroom floor is uneven, or could it be the extra bracelet I was wearing? Maybe it was the way I was standing on it, the dangling earrings, or the way I boofed my hair? I mean, hair gel and hair product have to weigh something, right? I looked at the number on the digital screen and shook my head in disgust. Then I proceeded to do just what I have done so many times before... I removed the dangling earrings, took off the cuff bracelet, repositioned the scales, undressed and weighed myself once more. To my surprise the number didn't change. Frustrated and full of anger, I went into my room, began to re-dress, slid on my high-heels, and headed out the front door slamming it fiercely behind me. Ughhh!

## I Am So Much More Than a Number

I allowed the number on that scale to dictate my morning, send my day into an unholy tizzy, and haunt my mind like a stray yard dog with a frenzy of insecurities and distorted thoughts of worthlessness. I felt shackled to that scale when the number went up even by an ounce. I had been oh so fickle with my self-worth, denying who I truly was in Christ, and granting Satan the power to use it to attack at my self-confidence.

For so long, I had chosen to believe the enemy's lies: *you're not smart enough, not pretty enough, you'll never lose the weight, and you might as well give up in defeat...* Not anymore! That scale had been my *go to*. I ran to it for affirmation in the morning, noontime, and even before bedtime. **I shamefully and sinfully stood on it more than I stood on the promises of God!** It was almost as if I was having an affair with the bathroom scale. I realized my bad habit had to go. It was time for me to take a stand against the enemy, pull out my dragon slaying weapons, fight through the power of Jesus, and take hold once and for all of the enemy's lies, sending them spiraling right back to the pits of hell where they came from!

### R.I.P. Bathroom Scale: Goodbye Bad Habits

A sledge-hammer! I needed a sledge-hammer, or maybe I could just run over the scale with our vehicle, and bury it in the back of the woods. I would dress for the occasion, slip on my finest black jogging pants, grab a box of tissues to hold back my tears of grief, gather around the hole in the ground, and bury it three feet deep within the soil, singing a song of mourning in my best Sound of Music opera voice as I slowly covered it with dirt. Whatever I decided, I knew the scale had to go.

Within the blink of an eye, it was gone- *kaput, adios, sayonara, so long, don't come back*- gone! I promise you the act of getting rid of that scale was not nearly as eventful as this drama queen just described, but I want you to know I removed it from my home.

You see, I, Beverly Weeks, REFUSED to place my self-worth in the numbers found on my bathroom scale, my checking or savings account, or on what other people think of me. It was time for me to remind myself that *I am a child of the most high God. I am significant, I am fearfully and wonderfully made, I am the apple of my Father's Eye, I am beautiful, qualified, and called. I am all that MY GOD says I am!*

## Is God Calling You To Let Go Of Some Bad Habits?

You may be there now. Pornography, gossiping, food addiction, alcohol, drugs, lying, cutting...you have tried all you can do, done all that is within your power. You've failed and you feel defeated. You see firsthand the pain it's causing your family, spouse, loved ones, and friends. You ache, you weep in distress, longing to be set free. I am confident that God wants you to be free. He is calling you to let go.

## L.E.T. G.O.

**L: Learn** that it's not by your power, or even willpower, but only through THE POWER of Christ living within you that you will be able to overcome any addiction. No matter what the circumstance, if you try to do it through your own might and self-control, you will absolutely fail.

*"I can do all things through Christ who strengthens me."* **Philippians 4:13 (NKJV)**

**E: Educate** yourself on ways to be victorious over your addiction through godly resources, biblical counseling, and church support groups. Take small baby steps to exercise your faith. Perhaps it's time for you to pick up the phone and find out when the next support group meeting will be held, or boldly tell your drinking buddy that you're going to stop drinking. I believe God wants us to step out in faith and take action.

**T: Trust in God.** If you are battling with an addiction,

ask for God's help in overcoming it and He will provide. I'm here to tell you that our God knows exactly what you are going through, and He knows what you need! There has NEVER been a time in your life that God didn't know what you needed. You need to reach out to God and allow Him to have POWER over the addiction that is ravaging your body and soul and sending your mind in a whirlwind frenzy. If you continue to hold on tight to the addiction, God will not take it away from you–you have to give it to Him! Desire to change. DO YOU WANT TO BE HEALED?

*"Trust in the Lord with all your heart and lean not on your own understanding; in all your ways submit to him and he will make your paths straight."* **Proverbs 3:5-6 (NIV)**

**G: Give** all your setbacks, past failures, and disappointments to God and lay them at His feet.

**O: Obey God,** first through prayer and by reading His Word. His Word encourages you to surround yourself with godly people who will encourage and lift you up.

**What addiction are you trying to break? What bad habit do you need to LET GO? Isn't it time to surrender your will to God and let Him take charge?**

# The Blessing in Lila Mae's Story

*I* could hear the rapid pounding of her knuckles against the hard wood frame as she began to knock fiercely on my hotel room door. *"Housekeeping,"* she called out. I opened the door and ushered her inside. Lila Mae was her name, jovial, animated and full of laughs, yet deep within her was a painful secret from the past that she had kept discreetly hidden for many years...

Earlier in the week, I had found myself sitting in my over-stuffed comfy chair, emotionally drained, overwhelmed, and praying that God would slow me down, show me how to get some misplaced priorities in line, and lead me to greater opportunities to hear the hearts of broken people. Yet amidst the chaos, busyness, and fast paced schedule, I had not anticipated the opportunity would come so quickly.

*"Lila Mae, you got any toothbrushes on that fancy little cart of yours? While you're searching, girlfriend, I ain't gonna' lie, I sure would love to have a couple extra packs of that orange flavored tea. AND by the way, you sure do ROCK that fancy hairdo!"* My southern girl accent and corny sense of humor caught Lila Mae and her assistant Jackie by surprise.

## What a Blessing; Moved With Compassion

Instantly, we hit it off. It was like we had known each other since childhood. Lila Mae stunned me, knocked me clear off my size eight feet, and sent me into a cackling, giggling, snorting tizzy by yanking off her wig and offering to let me try it on. My roommate, Jennifer, and I entertained Lila Mae and Jackie for what seemed like hours, but in reality it was fleeting minutes. The four of us broke into laughter that I am certain could be heard all up and down the halls on our hotel floor.

I looked up at Lila Mae and with a holy boldness that could only come from God I asked her to share her story. Lila Mae's voice broke. I could feel the salty tears on my lips as she began to tell how she had been sexually assaulted and abused when she was in middle school by several male family members, which included her father and brother.

Later, she would miscarry and deliver a small baby while sitting alone, broken, and confused in a stale, secluded restroom.

Her crushing experiences had led her to a life of low self-worth, promiscuity, drugs, and poor choices. Years later, she found herself staying in a woman's shelter, desiring a new life and change.

Miraculously, in the midst of her shattered dreams and unbelievable circumstances, she found God! That's right, Lila Mae had asked Jesus to come into her heart and set her free from the bondages that had once held her captive to her horrific past.

## The Lesson (and Blessing!) In Lila Mae's Story

Our time ended with the four of us holding hands and praying together for a mighty move of God in the Lila Mae's and Jackie's lives. We cried out and asked God to open a door for Lila Mae to leave the shelter and find a place of her own. The Holy Spirit had used Lila

Mae to slow me down and remind me that life is about more than just me and my wants, my fears, and my problems. I was put here for a purpose–to love, show compassion, share the gospel, and encourage others.

Sadly, there are many others just like Lila Mae longing for someone to hear their story. The shock of broken hearts can be found among our family members, friends, co-workers, at the gym, in the grocery store check-out lines, at the local shopping malls, and even within our churches. There are those struggling with finances, a prodigal child, depression, addictions, broken homes and marriages; they are desperate for someone to offer a word of hope, encouragement, and let them know we care. Souls are dying right under the shadow of our church steeples and people are giving up without ever knowing the hope that can be found in Jesus.

**Today ask God to help you see others as He sees them.**

*Father God, give us a heart of compassion for the hurting and the lost. Through this heart of compassion, move us to become a part of what You are doing to take the gospel to broken people in our families, communities, on the job, and outside the walls of our churches.*

*Lord, we pray that Your love will be loosed in our hearts so that we may love and encourage those who feel as if they have lost all hope. This is Your heart. By Your grace, may it also be our heart. In the name of Jesus, we pray, Amen.*

***"Finally, all of you, be like-minded, be sympathetic, love one another, be compassionate and humble."*
1 Peter 3:8 (NIV)**

## Marriage: God Still Resurrects the Dead

*I* could hear the music playing on the overhead speakers. I began to fidget with my wedding ring, sliding it back and forth upon my index finger while anxiously waiting for the attorney to enter the room. The songs were quickly muffled by raging thoughts of daunting questions–the what ifs, the whys, and of course, the feelings of conviction from my swift decision to file for separation.

Could a temporary separation save our marriage? Would going through with this threat *make* my *husband* change? Deep down, did I truthfully even want my marriage to be saved? After all, I was already emotionally attracted to another man.

What had led me to this pivotal point of thinking that this meeting with the lawyer was my only recourse? I mean, I knew better. I had been raised in church all my life. I had heard how God hates divorce. Would this mean that now He would hate me?

### The Death of Our Marriage

Our marriage relationship was crumbling. Our priorities had gotten so out of line with kids, careers, church, activities, community service, and committees that it felt like my husband and I were merely living together as roommates.

My selfish desires and coveting, that greener grass syndrome, left me longing for what other couples had.

I found myself becoming intrigued with another man and I no longer held the will or the want to make my marriage work. Communication within our marriage had stifled and our strained conversations led to bitter words, harsh, abrupt shouting matches, followed by the sounds of screeching car tires.

Our marriage was dead. As a matter of fact, it was *"Lazarus been in the grave three days stankin' dead!"* I was flirting with sin and my husband was feeling defeated and frustrated from not being able to control our circumstances. In the eyes of the world, it appeared that our marriage was over.

You might be reading this right now and you can relate. You, too, have found yourself in the middle of this crazy cycle, and you wonder if things can or will ever get better. BUT let me assure you when GOD steps on the scene, **EVERYTHING** changes.

## C.P.R. For A Dying Marriage

**C: Communicate, Confess & Commit:** Not only had areas of trust been broken within our marriage, but we found ourselves dealing with an array of feelings. There was unresolved hurt, bitterness, anger, my desire to be loved, and his desire to be respected. In order for the healing to take place in our marriage, I first needed to confess my sin, including my emotional involvement with another man. I cried out for forgiveness not only to my husband, but to God.

There could be no more lies. There would be no room for hidden text, emails, or secrets. My husband and I held each other as we wept. For the first time, we listened to one another like never before, and we cried even more. The tears were followed by forgiveness, sought and generously granted on both sides.

From that day forward we committed to each other to NEVER again allow the word *divorce* to enter our vocabulary. Most importantly, we recommitted our marriage to God by determining in our hearts to make our marriage the priority it was meant to be and keep Christ in the center of our relationship. Those healing tears have been followed by years of new life and laughter.

**P: Pray Like Never Before**: I remember sitting on the end my bed one night with my head buried in my trembling hands. I shouted out to God my deepest, most secret, inner thoughts. *Oh God, I feel so ashamed. How could I have allowed myself to be attracted to another man? Father, forgive me. Lord, repair my broken marriage and heal the wounds that I have caused our two children. God, minister to our family, take away the hurts, calm the fears, and ease the pain that no one but You, Lord, can fathom we are feeling...*

Can I tell you that there is POWER when you call on the name of Jesus?! Through prayer, couples draw closer to God, angry hearts are softened, wisdom is granted, and trust is rebuilt.

**R: Reach Out:** Why is it that we, as Christians, tend to isolate ourselves when we are going through a struggle or are under a spiritual attack? Isolation is a deadly tool in the hand of the enemy. For so long, we were guilty of being plastic Christians. We never once reached out for counseling in our past. Maybe it was the fear of sharing our intimate details with a complete stranger.

There were times I felt dysfunctional, like we were the only couple with issues. I allowed Satan to attack my mind with doubts and feelings of worthlessness.

**Listen to me and receive this in the name of Jesus**: *It's okay for Christians to reach out for help.* My husband and I sought the help of godly counselors who in turn placed in our hands godly resources and held us biblically accountable for decisions within our marriage. AND as if that was not enough, God said *I am not only going to bring that marriage back to life, but I am going to use your story* to give hope to others that need a touch of that same resurrection power in their marriages!

My friend, He raised up Lazarus from the grave. His resurrection is the reason we celebrate EASTER. If He can conquer death, then surely our GOD has the power to breathe NEW life into your marriage or whatever circumstance in your life the enemy has set ought to destroy.

# People Pleasing Syndrome

*"It was a one-eyed, one-horned, flyin' purple people eater (One-eyed, one-horned, flyin' purple people eater) A one-eyed, one-horned, flyin' purple people eater... Sure looks strange to me (One eye?)"*

I was walking around my home sulking with tears in my eyes, and I changing the lyrics to that 1958 classic around just a bit. I found myself singing them out loud, *"**SHE** was a one eyed, one horned, flyin' purple **people pleaser**, one eyed, one horned, flyin' purple **people pleaser**..."* And I was directing those words straight at me! Yes, I have finally admitted it. There have been times that I have been guilty of wallering in the pit of what I call the ***People Pleasing Syndrome.***

**I don't know why it was so hard for me to write this. It is the one thing about myself that is so absolutely irritating to me.** I have seen it cause fear, attack my self-esteem, produce anxiety and unnecessary worry, and just being candid, I have seen in the past where I allowed it to bring sin into my life.

Yes, I said SIN! **When you believe man's opinion of yourself over God's Word and you seek to please people more than God, my friend, that is just plain SIN.** There goes my hot pink painted toes again–I just stepped all over them, and honeychild, I am gonna need a pedicure!

Can you relate to not being able to say "no" to commitments, committees, and volunteer projects because you don't want to cause any conflict? Or you don't want people to think badly about you? And then you've allowed all those priorities to interfere with your time with God, your spouse, and your family?

I reflect back, and shamefully there have been times in my past when I permitted *people pleasing* to alter my personality. I am sure that I have looked *one eyed and one horned and every shade of purple!*

I remember one evening in particular, gathering at a restaurant table with a group of what I would call *influential and popular* ladies in the community. I was sharing the fake laughter, listening to their profanity and flirtatious remarks, yet I was seeking their approval and trying so hard to fit in with the 'in' crowd. I was ignoring all along that God did not want me to be in that SIN and that place to start with!

I look back and I have even changed things in my life to suit man's agenda. I was ignoring what the Holy Spirit had planned for my life! For too long, I was enslaved to it, feeding off the approval and affirmation that I received from others. I have actually tossed and turned in bed at night, filled with anxiety. *"Why doesn't she like me? What can I do to change it? What do they think of me? What does this person think or that person think?"* It was not until I cried out to God and said **"Father God, I need You to heal me of this disease, this desire to please others, instead of pleasing YOU"** that I was able to break free!

I am Beverly Weeks. I am fearfully and wonderfully made. I am funny, I have a big trunk, an extra belly roll, and a few sprigs of gray on the top. I am spontaneous, creative, and have been known to stick my foot in my mouth. I mess up and have been known to cry out to God in rage and fall to my knees and seek forgiveness. **I refuse to live for nothing less than what my GOD has in store for me!**

*"Am I now trying to win the approval of human beings, or of God? Or am I trying to please people? If I were still trying to please people, I would not be a servant of Christ."* **Galatians 1:10 (NIV)**

# Plastic Christians Fall

*H*e sat there on the side porch, holding his loafers in his hands; his hair prematurely graying from the sleepless nights, stress, and depression, which were taking their toll. I stood there in the doorway filled with resentment and bitterness and unwilling to share an ounce of compassion for him.

I tried to ignore my husband's presence, yet my eyes shifted, drawn to his bare feet and the tears falling uncontrollably from his tired eyes. ***"I want my family back. I want to come home. Please let me in."*** For several months, against my husband's will, we had lived apart. Our children were broken and confused after being shuffled from place to place. I had selfishly reached a point that I no longer possessed the will or desire to see it survive.

Communicating with each other had turned into nothing more than what seemed like a Wrestle Mania shouting match. I was mentally exhausted from crying and verbally defending my selfish decisions. Entangled emotionally with a male friend and flirting with sin, I justified our marriage separation, although very painful to everyone involved, would surely lead to happier times in the future for the both of us.

You know what was baffling? We both had been raised in church all our lives. We had held leadership positions, taught Sunday school, been involved in the choir and dramas. When we walked into church, we appeared to have it all together–a nice home, successful jobs, beautiful kids, and financial security. We had the perfect fake, plastic smiles and handshakes to masquerade the fears and hurts from a marriage that had turned to isolation, disrespect, and mixed up priorities. Yet deep down, we were broken, frustrated, filled with unforgiveness, and felt all alone.

**Can I get real with you?** As a couple, reaching out for help was one of the hardest things we ever had to do. You know, it seemed as if we had always been led as Christians to compress the hurt, hide the pain, and never let anyone in the church see or sense our failures. Our marriage looked good from the outside. Our neighborhood and church would have never guessed that we were struggling. We became experts at putting on a front.

My husband and I never once realized on our own what I am about to share with you...

**There are NO perfect marriages. There are NO perfect Christians.**

Your deacons, Sunday school teachers, and even your pastors mess up from time to time. Deep down, at the end of the day, everyone still has hurts, disappointments, and frustrations; everyone sins and fails God. That sin can lead to brokenness, loneliness, and can even lead you down a path of shameful regrets, **BUT** it's okay to let it lead you to a place where you realize you cannot walk it out alone. A place where you have to say, *we don't have all the answers, we don't have it all together, we just need help.*

Maybe you are at a point where I was years ago. It was embarrassing for us to share our junk with our pastor. I want you to know that is fine, as long as you reach out! Reach out to a godly counselor, a pastor at another church, or a godly friend. Whatever you do reach OUT! Somewhere along the way we, as Christians, have gotten the idea that is wrong to ask for help, that it is wrong to show there is nothing less than perfection within our churches.

Desperate, my husband and I reached out to godly marriage counselors who in turn showed us there was more to love and marriage than a whole bunch of bottled up fickle feelings. Our counselors showed us the biblical truths about marriage, encouraged us to pray together, worship together, and empowered us to attend marriage events/getaways that allowed for healing and restoration. There are times when we have to lay down our pride and realize that we cannot do it alone.

To resist temptation, make wise decisions and get back up when you have been knocked down. There will be times you when you have to lay aside the pride and ask for help.

*"Where there is no guidance, a people falls, but in an abundance of counselors there is safety."* **Proverbs 11:14 (ESV)**

# Tired? I'm Plumb Wore Out!

*I* don't think a hot stone massage or a Calgon bubble bath could begin to ease this exhaustion. A deep, intense, two-day sleep, or a rest in a hammock on a secluded island with a half a jar of peanut butter, a couple of coconuts and a chocolate bar nearby... hmmm maybe.

I'm tee-totally physically and mentally drained. It's one of those days where I find myself surrounded by the not so elegant scents and sights of two forever growing, endless piles of laundry. One is dirty and the other is just plain funky. Dirty means we can possibly wear it one more time. Funky means you better grab a gas mask and run just as fast as you can while loading it into the washer.

And then there's the kids–teenage tantrums, the tirades, an endless list of chores, emails, voicemails, activities, sports banquets, church activities, work, and end of the grade exams. Add a dash of supper duty, dirty toilets, dishes, and unmopped floors. Have I caused you to grab for the chocolate or have a nervous sugar meltdown? Honeychild, do you feel this drama momma's pain? Of course you do. We've all been there- tired, overcommitted, stressed, crazy schedules, drained, pulled in a million directions...

## Tired? It's Not Just Physical

I know all too well what it's like to feel the sting of

total emotional and spiritual exhaustion as well. Maybe you can relate. You find yourself begging and pleading with a child that has gone prodigal. You weep because you can't seem to make ends meet with a strained, failing budget, or maybe you find yourself in the battle of your life as you stand for your marriage. He has walked out on you. Your mind is being taunted with questions, the what ifs, the whys, the fear, doubt, and worry. Your heart tells you no one understands, the enemy tries to convince you that God doesn't hear your prayers, and that you are unseen and insignificant.

## Tired? God Is Calling You To Rest

Can I just get real with you? God is VERY interested in the topic of rest. To Him, rest is not just wasted time or time when we could be doing something useful and productive. Rest, in our Father's eyes, has value, worth, and purpose. We see in the Word of God that even Jesus rested. He often withdrew from people, ministry, and His daily routine in order to spend time alone with God.

*"...the news about him spread all the more, so that crowds of people came to hear him and to be healed of their sicknesses. But Jesus often withdrew to lonely places and prayed."* Luke 5:15-16 (NIV)

You see, Jesus understood that the need was endless. You may be sensing that same very thing as well. My children need me, my clients need me, my ailing parents need me, my friends need me, my husband needs me, work is calling my name... all the while our God is calling us to seek Him first, to get our priorities back in line, and find sweet rest.

*"Come to me, all you who are weary and burdened, and I will give you rest."* **Matthew 11:28 (NIV)**

**Finding R.E.S.T.**

**R: Renew** your mind, read the Word of God, and let your spirit be rejuvenated. I often love to camp out in the book of Psalms. It is there that many times, I find refuge and new strength to face my day-to-day battles.

**E: Escape** from your normal routine and daily pressures and get into the presence of God through prayer and meditation. Find a quiet place and take time to cry out to God. Our God sees your brokenness and your tears. He wants you to empty your exhaustion before Him.

**S: Surround** yourself with godly people who will encourage you. Sometimes the burdens are just too heavy to bear alone. God wants you to love and empower one another.

**T: Take** time for yourself! Exercise, take a walk, put your toes in the sand, find a new hobby, go shopping, do something for yourself, or grab that chocolate, peanut butter, and a couple of coconuts, before you go nuts!

**Are you stressed out, burned out and about to pull your hair out? There is only** One who can give you true rest–the refreshing, rejuvenating, restoring, refilling, life-giving rest that we all long for, and His name is Jesus.

# PORN: A Destructive Four Letter Word

*J*ust one innocent peek and no one will ever know... I tiptoed over to the coffee table and began to curiously unravel the crinkled up pages within the magazine. The photos were full of images of nudity and couples engaged in provocative sex acts. The articles and advertisements contained filthy, explicit language that I had never even heard of as a young teenager.

I was thirteen at the time and I had allowed my junior high friend to coerce me to take a quick look at the pages. *Just one peek...what harm could ever be caused?* My friend and I had been asked to babysit for a young couple with two small children. I was a little surprised that they had left the stacks of X-rated magazines lying around in full view.

The twisted images of sex were not at all what my naive mind had imagined. Everything was so visibly distorted, leaving me to believe for such a long time that sex was grossly overrated. It appeared to be such a nonchalant, ugly, ungodly thing. Pornography has a way of holding your mind captive to the toxic ideas of what sex really isn't.

## The Guilt & Shame

That night, as I was lying in bed, the pictures kept replaying over and over again in my head. I tried to get the dark, sinful impressions out of my mind. My uncontrolled thoughts and curiosity only made me feel more ashamed and full of conviction. What had led me to cave into the pressure from my friend? I knew better. I had been raised in church all of my life. Why was I so drawn to the lust filled images within those pages?

## Shocking Porn Facts

**Now more than ever Satan is on a rampage to destroy our homes.** He knows he can use this sinful tool to threaten lives, families, marriages, and children. Porn has become a damaging, life changing, destructive four letter word!

There is not a week that goes by that someone in our ministry doesn't have to reach out to a couple or family that has been affected by this looming, powerful, devastating industry. What came as a major surprise to me, however, was to learn that pornography revenue is larger than the revenues of all professional football, baseball, and basketball franchises COMBINED! Friends we need to wake up, porn is a huge problem!

### *More Alarming Facts from xxxchurch.com:*

*35% of all internet downloads are pornographic*

*43% of all internet users view pornographic material (1 out of 3 are female)*

*For every 10 men in church, 5 are struggling with pornography*

*Sex & porn are among the 5 top search terms for kids under 18*

*The average age of first internet exposure and pornography is 11 years old*

*Half of all hotel guests order pornographic movies*

*38% of adults think it is morally acceptable to look at pictures of nudity and sexual behavior*

*The pornography industry, according to conservative estimates, brings in $57 billion per year, of which the United States is responsible for $12 billion.*

**What can you do?**

Do you want to be set free from the bondage of pornography and sexual sin? My friend, you cannot do it alone. Pornography addiction is one of the most difficult addictions to overcome. Even the secular world recognizes the power of the addiction and its effect on our children.

**Educate Yourself.** Ignorance is no excuse, so get armed for the battle. Xxxchurch.com is an incredible resource and has proven helpful when mentoring couples who have found themselves right smack dab in the middle of a fiery attack on their marriage from the pain, distrust, lies, and hurt associated with porn. Email me at Beverly@intentionallyyours.org and I will send you articles for encouragement.

These two books by Stephen Arterburn are excellent resources: Every Man's Battle for men and Every Heart Restored for the women who want to understand the battle their husbands are born into and come alongside them to help them win the battle for their eyes and hearts.

**Don't do it alone.** Find yourself an accountability partner– someone who will walk alongside you while you are battling with this struggle. This may be your spouse, a friend, or a minister. Accountability is the critical first step to any recovery journey. Since most porn use is now online, it's crucial to get the best monitoring and filtering software available. If you're serious about avoiding porn or recovering from porn addiction, it all starts with accountability, and inviting someone to walk alongside you in this battle.

# What to do When Your Marriage is Falling Apart

*H*is voice began to break as he shouted above the roar of the blaring vacuum cleaner. *"Tell me, I have to know, do you still love me?"* I ignored the impending question. His tone became stronger, and the look of fear and concern became more evident in his temples and tear-filled brown eyes. My selfish desires had led me to a life that was flirting and dabbling with secret sin. I looked up at my husband and blurted out, *"I just don't feel a thing..."*

**How had we become so distant?** Our marriage was falling apart; it had become a relationship filled with disrespect, mixed up priorities and poor communication. We'd been engrossed in our careers, kids, and invested our time, energy and efforts into everything and everyone except our floundering marriage. We had grown complacent, distant, fallen prey to the enemy's distractions, and reached the point that we were merely living together as roommates.

For so long, I secretly longed for my husband's affection, a gentle kiss, hug, or even a whispered, *I love you.* My husband's not understanding or meeting my needs, my lingering insecurities, and my distant relationship with God, left me harboring bitter feelings, unforgiveness, compressed hurts, and raw emotions. Our marriage became stale, broken, and lifeless...it was falling apart.

**R.O.A.D. To Restoration When Your Marriage is Falling Apart**

Maybe you find yourself there–traveling on that same broken road that my husband and I were on years ago. Devastation surrounds you, threatening your marriage, and you feel as if you can't take it anymore. Perhaps it's the pain of an emotional or sexual affair that has been exposed, the perversion of pornography, the hurts from lies, disrespect, an addiction, a conflict with in laws, children, finances... the list goes on.

## My marriage was falling apart

What do you do when your marriage is falling apart, being swallowed up by the waves of doubt, fear, and dishonesty? Or if you are haunted by assumptions, and the threat of separation or a divorce looms on the horizon?

**R: Repent & Realize:** Repentance has to come before restoration can take place in any relationship. My husband and I both had to seek forgiveness first from God, and then from each other. You see, according to the Word of God, forgiveness is not optional.

*"Bear with each other and forgive one another if any of you has a grievance against someone. Forgive as the Lord forgave you."* **Colossians 3:13 (NIV)**

**Realize that this is not a fight against your spouse**, but it is very much an all out spiritual warfare the enemy has waged in an effort to destroy your marriage, family and your home. That arrogant, pesky, slime bag Satan would like nothing more than to invade your home, create confusion, cause busyness, and put a wedge between you and your spouse. He wants to rock the very core of your marriage, sending it hightailing off its foundation.

*"For we wrestle not against flesh and blood, but*

*against principalities, against powers, against the rulers of the darkness of this world, against spiritual wickedness in high places."* **Ephesians 6:12 (KJV)**

**O: Obey God:** A marriage will not succeed without first maintaining your individual relationships with God. This obedience comes through prayer, knowing the Word of God, seeking godly counsel and resources, and reaching out to friends who will hold you accountable.

**A: Affirm Your Spouse:** It's time to stop tearing one another down! Be slow to speak, quick to listen, and slow to anger.

*"My dear brothers and sisters, take note of this: Everyone should be quick to listen, slow to speak and slow to become angry."* **James 1:19 (NIV)**

**D: Determine to Stand for Your Marriage:** Don't base your reactions on what you see or feel. Determine that come hell or high water, high winds or the point of destruction, that you will stand for your marriage in obedience to God, and you will not give up, give in, give out or give over 'til healing takes place. *As long as you are breathing, there is hope.* Our God is still raising the dead to life, and that includes YOUR marriage! And it includes your friend's marriage. Will you stand with us?

*I AM STANDING FOR THE HEALING OF MY MARRIAGE!*

*I will not give up, give in, give out or give over 'til that healing takes place. I made a vow, I said the words, I gave the pledge, I gave a ring, I took a ring, I gave myself, I trusted GOD, said the words, and meant the words... in sickness and in health, in sorrow and in joy, for better or for worse, for richer or for poorer, in good times and in bad. So I am standing NOW, and will not sit down, let down, slow down, calm down, fall down, look down or be down 'til the breakdown is torn down!*

*I refuse to put my eyes on outward circumstances, or listen to prophets of doom, or buy into what is trendy, worldly, popular, convenient, easy, quick, thrifty, or advantageous... nor will I settle for a cheap imitation of God's real thing, nor will I seek to lower God's standard, twist God's will, rewrite God's Word, violate God's covenant, or accept what God hates, namely divorce!*

*In a world of filth, I will stay pure; surrounded by lies I will speak the truth; where hopelessness abounds, I will hope in God: where revenge is easier, I will bless instead of curse; and where the odds are stacked against me, I will trust in God's faithfulness.*

*I am a STANDER, and I will not acquiesce, compromise, quarrel or quit. I have made the choice, set my face, entered the race, believed the Word, and trusted God for all the outcome.*

*I will allow neither the reaction of my spouse, nor the urging of my friends, nor the advice of my loved ones, nor economic hardship, nor the prompting of the devil to make me let up, slow up, blow up, or give up 'til my marriage is healed.*

*- Author Unknown*

# Shattered Dreams

*H*ave you ever had one of those mornings, days, weeks, months, or even years when it felt like all of hell was breaking loose? Seeing your dreams shattered? I'm talking about frustrating, mind-boggling, hair pulling, earth shattering situations that crept into your life and wreaked havoc over your home, finances, marriage, relationships, job–shattering your dreams and knocking you tee-totally slam off your size seven feet? Maybe it was an unexpected doctor's report, bankruptcy, or the anxiety and worry that accompanies standing for a prodigal spouse or child that has turned away from Jesus? Perhaps it was a violent attack of gossip, depression, worry, anxiety, or fear?

No matter what the circumstance, when you find yourself right smack dab in the middle of what seems like hell's blazing fury, and the flames seem to be overtaking you and it's all you can do to keep from smothering to death from the stench of everything you've ever held dear in your life being consumed by the enemies darts, it's time to STAND on the promises of GOD, call on reinforcements and yell out to the top of your lungs, ***GET THEE BEHIND ME SATAN!***

## Shattered Dreams: Sometimes Life Is Just Not Fair

Just pick up the Sunday paper, turn on the news, and gather around the breakfast table at a local diner–the stories can seem so unreal and devastating. People shot and killed for no reason, a missing airplane, drug dealers peddling their poison like candy to our teenagers and small children, hurricanes destroying homes and taking lives–suffering and pain happens.

I have seen it in my own family. I watched helplessly as my husband wept and stood by the gravesite of his brother who was tragically electrocuted years ago, taken away at such a young age from his two small children. I have gazed upon the eyes of my mother as she fought to take a breath after being horribly injured and disfigured in a car accident. I knelt beside my mother-in-law as she cried out in anguish, breast cancer attacking her small frame and causing great pain in her bones and all over her body.

I saw firsthand the fear that rested upon my husband's face for months as I was running from God. I had selfishly disregarded my family, our marriage, and our home for short-lived, sinful pleasures.

## Shattered Dreams: Sometimes It Makes No Sense

I sat in my car counseling a young girl who shared with me the horrible, vile story of how she had been sexually assaulted. Her attackers had not only stripped her of her dignity, but they had left her frightened, confused, numbed, and had stolen her will to live.

My eyes filled with tears as I ran my fingers across the fresh scars where she had cut her wrist and tried to end her life. She went on to tell me how she was now facing an unwanted pregnancy, and trembled as she explained the guilt, the hurt, and frustrations. She felt so bitter, so confused, and all alone.

I have seen people go through some of the worst

experiences possible. I have seen people endure hardships that would cause a common person to crumble and give up. I have seen people stand in the midst of shear chaos. You know what I am talking about. You may even be living it now! Your spouse may have walked out on you, there may have been the revelation of an affair, the heart-break of pornography, your family has been broken, your dreams shattered... And now you are left holding the broken pieces.

## We Have An Enemy

*"You see, our enemy is not of flesh and blood, but against forces and authorities and against rulers of darkness and powers in the spiritual world."* **Ephesians 6:12**

How do we survive the attacks of the enemy? We must recognize that although he is powerful, Satan's powers are limited. The believer who lives by the Spirit of God can resist the enemy's attacks. I don't know about you, but honeychild, sometimes I would love to pull out a pair of my three-inch spiked heels, stomp all over the devil, kick his ugly self right back to the pits of hell where he came from, shouting, '**take your nastified, unglorified paws off of me and my family!!**'

## We've Got The Power In The Name of Jesus

There's a song we used to sing at church that goes like this: *"We've got the power in the name of Jesus, we've got the power in the name of the Lord, though Satan rages **we cannot be defeated**, we've got the power in the name of the Lord."*

I want you to know that attacks will come, there will be days that you have to fight with all of your might, but you never have to do it alone. There is **power** when we stand on the promises found in the Word of God. There is **power** when you speak scripture. I can tell you that the enemy cringes and his demons start itching. They can't stand it!

There is **power** when you fall to your knees and cry out to God in prayer. There is **power** when you call on your church community and godly friends and surround yourself with Christian men and women who will stand with you so you don't have to fight your battle alone. No matter how grim your situation may look, OUR GOD is on His throne and there is **POWER** when you call on His name!

*"Finally, be strong in the Lord and in his mighty power. Put on the full armor of God so that you can take your stand against the devil's schemes. For our struggle is not against flesh and blood, but against the rulers, against the authorities, against the powers of this dark world and against the spiritual forces of evil in the heavenly realms.*

*Therefore put on the full armor of God, so that when the day of evil comes, you may be able to stand your ground, and after you have done everything, to stand. Stand firm then, with the belt of truth buckled around your waist, with the breastplate of righteousness in place, and with your feet fitted with the readiness that comes from the gospel of peace.*

*In addition to all this, take up the shield of faith, with which you can extinguish all the flaming arrows of the evil one. Take the helmet of salvation and the sword of the Spirit, which is the word of God." Ephesians 6:10-17 (NIV)*

# She Ain't Right, Bless Her Heart!

*I*t was the million dollar, unexpected, kids say the darndest things question, that in all my years of motherhood, I had tee-totally not prepared myself for. To make things even worse, I was standing there with the dreaded bed head, absolutely no makeup, no Spandex, no peanut butter or dark chocolate to grab for refuge, and not an ounce of caffeine in sight.

I leaned against the counter in my camisole and gazed into the vanity mirror. The words that my naive little 8-year-old daughter had so innocently just blurted out resonated in my ears, knocked my Betty Bouffant bangs down, viciously attacked my insecurities, and haunted me like a growling stray dog: *"Mama, how come most people's muscles go up on top of their arms, but yours fall down?"*

At that very moment, there was not one ounce of vanity left anywhere in my body. In all honesty, I felt completely unattractive. My entire disposition and personality began to change. For the rest of the morning, I was guilty in the first degree of the sinful *woe is me* sulking. The enemy had me right where he wanted me.

## Falling Prey To The Comparison Trap

Have mercy, this is the part where this southern girl gets real. I can hear someone now chuckling around the water cooler as you shout out, *"She ain't right.*

116

*Bless her heart!"*

You see, I had allowed Satan to attack my mind and suck me into the violent trap of the comparison syndrome. Oh, if I only had her legs, or her figure, her smile, her tan, her lean arms; and my attitude led to a gloomy morning. It affected the way I reacted toward my husband when he tried to touch me or even compliment me.

## I'm Not The Only One

Sadly, over half of the women reading this would say that they don't feel beautiful. I get angry and foot stompin', gray hair turning mad that we, as women, have allowed the world's standard of beauty to become our standards, determine our self-worth, and effect the way we feel about ourselves. Ouch, here I go, stepping all over my toes!

Yes, I admit that I, too, have been guilty of being held captive by the enemy's lies–the mind boggling, thought provoking, you just don't measure up untruths that come straight from the pits of hell!

I remember once being on the computer and I could not help but stare at some of the photos on a friend's Facebook page. Never mind that this individual was much younger than me. I just kept thinking about how incredibly beautiful she looked and how she appeared to have it all together. Tan skin, wavy thick brown hair, absolutely no wrinkles, fine lines, or circles, and not one thing on her body appeared to sag or drag. I bet the word cellulite had never even been introduced into her vocabulary. I found myself trapped in envy and falling prey to the sinful coveting and comparison syndrome.

**You know placing our self-worth in the world's**

**standards is one of the very reasons we, as women and wives, have not allowed ourselves to feel beautiful**. Just walk through any checkout line at the supermarket. Everything is airbrushed, cropped, chopped, Photoshopped, and blemish free. It's fake and we allow it to undermine our sense of beauty. We compare our worst days to someone else's best days.

## Insecurities In The Bedroom

In my past, I have been guilty of allowing my insecurities to affect my intimacy within my marriage. For so long, I was uncomfortable with my husband seeing me unclothed or even touching me unless the lights were turned out.

Ladies, my husband can send his laundry out to be dry cleaned, have his dinner prepared at a restaurant, confide his deepest secrets with a buddy, and in doing all these things he is still in the will of God. If my husband has sex with anyone other than his wife, he is in sin!

I was so insecure in who I was in Christ, that I allowed the enemy to have that stronghold in my life. Our husbands want to be intimate with us. They desire that affirmation from their wife.

## Set Your Heart Free

**How does one break away from this bondage?** I have tearfully come to recognize that it is only through the earth rattling, life changing power of Jesus Christ and through fervent prayer that you can be delivered.

There are days that I have to begin my morning by taking control of my thoughts and saying, "*God, today I am struggling in this area, and I need You to help me. Father, help me to be content, and remind me that I am fearfully and wonderfully made. Lord, thank you that I am chosen. With you I am confident."*

You see, this wife has put her stake in the ground. I refuse to let Satan toss darts of lies and insecurities as a means to interfere in my marriage. There is a verse that I have grown to cherish in this battle:

**"Before I formed thee in the belly I knew thee; and before thou camest forth out of the womb I sanctified thee..." Jeremiah 1:5 (KJV)**

How awesome is that? My God loves me, not because of what I am, or what I've done, or what size I am, but because of **Whose** I am. I am **HIS** and He loves me and all my imperfections. I am beautiful: dimples, freckles, rounded hips, even my junk in the trunk... it was all fearfully and wonderfully made by Him!

# SHO NUFF, I've Done Flunked Motherhood

*I*t was a week full of demanding work schedules, speaking engagements, sports, church, kids' activities, bad news, and the onslaught of a severe case of *People Pleasing Syndrome.* I had just about managed to pluck out every protruding, scraggly, gray hair that was left standing catty-wampus on my head. Everything and everyone seemed to get on my last nerve. There were unanswered emails, voicemails, texts, committee meetings, Facebook messages, and a To Do List that would stretch from the top of a fifteen story high-rise building to the basement.

## Feelings of Failure in Motherhood

Why couldn't I get it together? I felt like a complete momma failure. I mean, all the other moms bake gourmet home cooked meals, AND they change their bed sheets every two days. It seemed I could barely even manage to wash or change our bed linens once a month.

Feeling determined, I resolved that I would at least separate our endless mound of laundry into two piles. There was dirty, and then there was funky. Dirty meaning we could possibly wear it ONE more time, and funky meant you better grab a gas mask and RUN just as fast as you can while loading it.

In all honesty, the sense of defeat had left me feeling overwhelmed, burdened, unappreciated, and feeling so insignificant.... I thought to myself, *Sho'Nuff I've done flunked motherhood!*

## The Enemy's Lies

Have you ever noticed how that cotton pickin', good for nothing enemy likes to take a strike at you and whip up on your insecurities when your life is overwhelmed, filled with chaos from the busyness, and your priorities are out of line?

Satan wants to bombard your thoughts with his pesky, poisonous darts so that you feel like you can't take it anymore; like you have surely messed up, will never get it right, and that you have become a genuine, fortified momma loser. The devil is a liar!

If not careful, we can become so exhausted and full of stress that we undoubtedly begin to flirt with depression, give in to attacks, feast on and believe in the enemy's lies. Pretty soon we find ourselves entertaining them as truth.

*"Cast all your anxiety on him because he cares for you. Be alert and of sober mind. Your enemy the devil prowls around like a roaring lion looking for someone to devour." 1 Peter 5:7-8 (NIV)*

## The Real Moment of Truth

Your failures, weaknesses, and the sin of being overcommitted and overwhelmed is not who you are. I have come to fully recognize that God is glorified when I admit my failures, and when I turn to Him for help.

There are times that I have to go to Him and say, *Father God, I need You to help me with this pride and arrogance in my heart, this desire to be a people*

121

*pleaser, and my sin of misplaced priorities. I need your grace, wisdom and divine strength. Lord, soften my rough edges and help me to set my eyes on you. Order my steps and my thoughts today.*

## M.O.M.

So what do you do as a mom when you feel like you are tee-totally losing it?

The toilets have all overflowed, the fungus from the spilt baby milk and dry cereal has grown into the carpet pattern, all the white underwear have turned pink from being washed with your favorite red blouse, the only vegetable you have served your kids the entire week is the all American potato in the form of a high fat French-fry, and you feel like surely if you were graded by your college professor you would receive a whopping F minus for your momma skills.

**M: Manage Your Thoughts** - That's right, take control of your thoughts! Think on things that are true, pure, holy, right, excellent, and praiseworthy. You are a great mom! You are learning and growing. With Christ on your side, there is absolutely, positively, nothing that you are not capable of doing.

**O-Obey God-** Through prayer and by taking time to slow down, get alone with our Father and refresh your spirit through praying and reading God's Word.

**M: My God Sees Me** – Remember your God is a God who sees and hears. You can be assured that He hears the words we utter. They may be uttered out of despair, out of a need, a pressing momma crisis, or they may be uttered out of praise and thanksgiving. He sees and hears our deepest moaning and groanings. When you find your mind being wracked with doubts and worries, take heart that our God knows what you are concerned about.

# Trusting GOD with Broken Finances

*"You want us to do what? Are you kidding me, momma? You want us to pray around the mailbox? I just gotta know one thing, have you lost it or joined a cult or something? Do you know what the neighbors will think if they see us praying around our mailbox?*

My thirteen year old son did not know whether to laugh or run, but at that time I knew God was leading me to have the *faith* to gather my family around our mailbox to pray for some **BOLD** things to happen in our home.

Earlier that week, I was forced to leave my job because of circumstances beyond my control. At the same time, my husband and I had been praying for God to open new doors in ministry. I could not comprehend how leaving my job so quickly could even be a part of God's plan. On top of that, my boss had written a letter to deny the unemployment.

**At that time anxiety and worry began to kick in full force.** My mind was being attacked by the what ifs, darts of fear, and the how would we financially make it questions. I had no other choice but to say *GOD, I need You to STEP onto the scene!*

Have you ever been in a situation so desperate that you knew, without a doubt, there was **NO way out BUT GOD?**

My husband and I gathered our children around that

mailbox, and we prayed and cried out to God for what seemed like an hour. *"Father, You own the cattle on a thousand hills, the wealth in every mine, and we are asking You to have mercy on Your children. God, we need You to take control of the situation with the unemployment and have financial favor on our family. We know You did not bring us this far into ministry for us to fail!"* We even started to pray for the junk mail. That's right! I knew that God could bless us with coupons and promotions to help lower our expenses.

A few weeks passed. One morning, I was online paying our bills when I stopped to look at the balance in our account, which was puzzling. How could I have paid the bills and *still* have money in the account? I immediately called up our bank to speak with a service representative to explain the situation. She explained that the money was *real, and yes, it was ours.* The Employment Security Commission had direct deposited a check into our account! I broke out in tears. The service representative probably thought I had lost my mind, so I explained to her how God had not only showed up, BUT showed off, and that this was a result of our family praying some mighty BIG BOLD prayers. We were having church right there on the telephone!

Not only did God reverse the decision with the unemployment, but friend, His favor did not stop there. We received a statement from childcare. I was keenly aware that I would need to pay $500 for its services for that month–however, the invoice read that we overpaid and they owed us money! How awesome is that?

Let's not forget the prayer for the junk mail...within days I opened two letters from an insurance company to shred and looked inside. I broke out in a glory

125

dance for JESUS–there were two unexpected refund checks! That glory dance caused me to bruise a few things and swing a hip or two out of place but that is a whole notha' story! For a little while, I felt no pain. I just knew MY GOD had heard my cry and He had come through.

**God had it all under control even before we breathed the first word of those prayers**. He just needed me to have the *faith* **to trust HIM** to work this out.

Are you in the middle of a crisis? Is it your broken finances, a broken marriage, illness, a prodigal child? My heart breaks for the many couples we have spoken with who are struggling in their marriage because of financial hardships. Friend, there will be times that you just have to fall to your knees, and cry out to God, saying, *"Lord, for the mortgage, for the car payment, for the credit card bills, doctor bills, whatever it is...* ***GOD, I trust You!"***

# When the Grass Looks Greener on the Other Side

**W**hy is it sometimes within our MARRIAGES, the grass can *APPEAR* to look greener on the other side? We get our priorities so out of line–work, kids, church, sports, commitments–that we soon forget to communicate, to take time for each other, to water *OUR* own lawns. We find ourselves enticed to the sights–oh, if I could just have that lifestyle, enchanted and drawn to the sounds of a flirtatious remark, or allured by the feeling you had when you received that compliment from a man or woman other than your spouse.

If our hearts are left unguarded, it can lead to coveting, complaining, discontentment, and soul-draining, relationship-killing envy. You see there was a time in my marriage many years ago that I became shackled to discontentment. It lead to self pity, anger, depression and self-centeredness. If we are not careful, we can find ourselves right smack dab in the middle of falling into a death trap of sins such as devastating emotional or sexual affairs. Yes, *I was that prodigal wife.*

## Don't Be Fooled, Every Marriage Has Weeds

My friend, no matter what you think, **EVERY** marriage has weeds! Your neighbor's marriage, your church deacons', your Sunday school teachers', even your pastor's marriage. No one is exempt. It is unrealistic to believe that you can live with another human being

127

for any length of time without having relationship problems.

## Tend The Lawn: P.R.U.N.E. to Get Rid of the Weeds

**P: Pray for your spouse.** Praying together as a couple and praying individually for your spouse are the most powerful weapons you have against attacks from the enemy. Two of my favorite books to help you form a plan are by Stormie O'Martian, *Power of a Praying Husband* and *Power of a Praying Wife*. These books changed our lives, marriage, and legacy.

**R:** Rid your marriage of the unrealistic expectations. You need to realize that your spouse can not meet your **EVERY** need–he wasn't created to. There is only One who can do that and His name is **JESUS**!!

**U: Uninterrupted couch time.** Take at least 15 minutes of communicating with your spouse without the distraction of electronics, kids, and the remote control...every day. That's right, we need to make time to listen to each other every day.

**N: Needed accountability.** We all need Christian friends to hold us accountable in our marriages. Are your friends telling you only what you want to hear? If you are struggling in your marriage, you need to be cautious about who you are taking advice from. If the words being whispered in your ear do not line up with the Word of God, you need to run from them.

**E: Enjoy regular date nights.** We all have insanely busy lives. Couples need to reconnect emotionally and physically on a regular basis. Go ahead, write those date nights on a calendar and tape it to the refrigerator. Go dancing, to the movies, to the dollar store, go parking–whatever you do, use your imagination, laugh, and have fun. Just GO, GO, GO!

You see sometimes the grass looks greener and we just need to water our OWN lawns. I love the realization that sometimes the grass looks greener because you can't see the *MANURE* from where you are standing! Think about that one...

*"Put to death, therefore, whatever belongs to your earthly nature: sexual immorality, impurity, lust evil desires and greed, which is idolatry."*
**Colossians 3:5 (NIV)**

# The Comparison Pit: Who Had I Become?

*"You don't love me anymore, do you?"* I could hear the frustration in my husband's voice as he shouted loudly above the vacuum cleaner. Refusing to acknowledge his question, I continued to proceed with the cleaning. He jerked the cord from the wall, and with tears flowing down his cheeks, he approached me, then blurted it out once more. *"Please answer me, I have to know. Do you still love me?"*

My marriage was collapsing and I was becoming someone I did not even recognize. Looking back, I can see where I had fallen deeply into the sin of coveting. There, I said it. It is still painful to share. I was guilty of coveting. I had become self-centered, seeking to fulfill my own forbidden, selfish desires and almost allowing them to destroy my family.

Just being candid, it took me quite some time to understand that my bondage to what I call the *comparison syndrome* had led to such a crippling sin in my life. I was longing and desiring to feel beautiful. I realize now that I was basing my standards on nothing more than the fake standards of beauty placed on women every day. We see it on the air brushed pages of every magazine in the grocery store checkout line, on television, the big screen, billboards, and even on social media. Not many people post unflattering profile pics. Oh, I am not judging. Believe me, girlfriend, I love that crop feature better than anyone. It's invaluable when my derriere is hanging out too far; I just crop it off!

## Pit of Comparison

I mean, let's get real. In most cases, you will not see a size 12 model on the front page of a magazine. And if you do, her cellulite is not showing, unlike mine! There are no signs of the fine lines, sagging boobs, or dark circles. It's all cropped, chopped, and airbrushed perfectly. For too long, I allowed Satan to take up space in my mind with thoughts of a low sense of worth and brutal attacks of low self-esteem. The true, sad fact was I had fallen into the pit of comparing my weaknesses to others strengths!

You see, my motivations to look beautiful turned sinful when I allowed them to be so strong that I started to covet the legs *she* had, the firm hiney *she* had, the toned tummy *she* had, *her* tanned skin or even her perfect hair. Even more destructive are the desires for the fun party life *she* lived, the fun trips, or the perceived *perfect exciting marriage* that someone else enjoyed. I remember sitting at a restaurant table one night with what I call well-to-do, popular, newly separated ladies. I tried the giggles, the fake laughs, and flirts with the men sitting nearby. I knew it was wrong for me to be in that place. It was all just a lie. **Who had I become?**

Desperate to salvage my marriage and break free from the chains of low self-esteem and insecurities, I found myself weeping frantically one night in the wee hours at the end of my bed. ***Oh God, I need you. I cannot do this on my own. My marriage has fallen to pieces, I feel ugly, confused, unheard, insignificant, and I am ready to be free. I need YOU to change my ATTITUDE. Take away this hurt, my fears of rejection, and feelings of low***

*self-worth. Father, I need You to show me who*
*You created me to be. Help me to trust You.*

Oh yes, I gave the devil a fierce, harsh, crushing blow
that night! **I refuse to allow myself to fall into that**
**pattern of thinking ever again.** I know I messed
up Satan's plans big time. I am sure he was out to
slowly kill me and destroy my home. I praise God for
healing my marriage and setting me free from this
bondage.

I won't lie to you, it's not easy. I wish I could tell you
that I never fall into a comparison rut. I do know that
each morning, I have to pray for God to direct my
thoughts, renew my mind, and if I find myself falling
prey to my insecurities, I cry out for God to change
my attitude.

# You Are Ugly: A Lie From Hell!

My eyes were fixed on the number on the scale. How could this have happened? 5'4" and over 240 pounds; for years, I had been eating just to fill the void. Working in a commission-only sales field definitely held its share of perks and stresses.

If I found myself under emotional stress, wondering where the next sales contract would come from or the next possible lead, I would turn to food as my comfort. On the contrary, if I landed a huge commission paycheck, the first thing I would do is reward myself with my favorite meal of steak, bread sticks, and Alfredo sauce.

## The Lies That Consumed Me

Years of poor healthy eating habits, binge eating, and yo-yo dieting wreaked havoc on my self-esteem. On top of that, I just did not feel beautiful. I found myself trapped inside a marriage of convenience. My insecurities held me in bondage; I did not feel desirable, loved, or esteemed by my husband. Sex held no pleasure for me; it merely became another chore. Our priorities were so out of line with kids, jobs, church activities, PTA, and other things. We were living together as roommates.

## The Chains Around My Neck

I found myself making excuses to just to stay at home and lounge around in my frumpy pajamas. The pain was so unbearable. I tried to hide my sense of low self-worth by always laughing at myself, being the life of the party, and carrying around the infamous fake smile. Yet at night, I would stand in front of the bathroom mirror, hold my face in my hands and silently weep. I just felt so ugly. Even worse, my looming insecurities had led to a life of coveting, jealousy, envy, self-loathing, and just plain outright sin!

The stress and poor nutrition had taken its toll on my body, and I began to lose my thick, wavy brown hair. I could remember removing what seemed liked handfuls of broken hair from the bottom of the shower. My pale skin was beginning to shine through my thinning crown. I had thrown away all confidence and chosen to stay in that dark pit, all the while allowing Satan's chains to be tightened around my neck, arms, and feet, nearly strangling the life out of me.

**The Power to Be Set Free**

**BUT THEN GOD!!** To realize that I, Beverly Weeks, could be set free from the bondage and chains that held me, to realize that I had the power in the Name of Jesus, to realize that I could cry out to GOD, that HE could empower me to think about my choices, to realize that I was His most valuable prized possession, that I am a child of the King, that I am loved, valued, and esteemed by Him, to realize that through His Holy Spirit I could be set free, to realize that I could pray and find the answers in God's Word **changed EVERYTHING!**

I want you to know that for years I looked in the mirror and consciously I chose to repeat the lie *you are ugly* in my head over and over again. By the power of Jesus, I have stomped and trampled all over that lie and sent it right back to the pits of hell where it came from!! I am FREE!

## You Will Be Tempted

Do I still struggle with my weight? Honeychild, I ain't gonna lie, the answer is yes. Do I still feel discouraged at times? Yes. DO I FEEL DEFEATED? NO, NO, NO!! It is then that I have to make the choice again. I can choose to stay in the valley of defeat, or I can go forth kicking and screaming and declaring that I am covered by the blood of Jesus and there is POWER in HIS name to break every chain.

## Do You Want To Be Set Free?

In what area of your life do you need to be set free? Are you in bondage to insecurity, a poor eating habit, a drug addiction, pornography, isolation, financial crisis, or a broken relationship? Are those chains strangling the life out of you? Don't wallow in those unhealthy emotions. TODAY IS YOUR DAY OF VICTORY! You can do this!

Don't allow your fears to fuel your insecurities. Cry out to God and share with Him your fears, struggles, and challenges. God is saying to you right now, *come to Me, all you who are weary and burdened, and I will give you rest!*

*"I sought the LORD, and He answered me: He delivered me from all my fears." Psalm 34:4 (NIV)*

# Part III

# Power Tools: God's Word for the Battle

# Preparing for Battle- There is POWER in Speaking God's Word!

## Scriptures from the New International Version (NIV)

I have given you authority to trample on snakes and scorpions and to overcome all the power of the enemy; nothing will harm you.
**Luke 10:19**

When you pass through the waters,
   I will be with you;
and when you pass through the rivers,
   they will not sweep over you
When you walk through the fire,
   you will not be burned;
   the flames will not set you ablaze.
**Isaiah 43:2**

I sought the Lord, and he answered me;
   he delivered me from all my fears.
**Psalm 34:4**

Do not conform to the pattern of this world, but be transformed by the renewing of your mind. Then you will be able to test and approve what God's will is— his good, pleasing and perfect will.
**Romans 12:2**

Cast all your anxiety on him because he cares for

you.
**1 Peter 5:7**

[18] "Forget the former things;
    do not dwell on the past.
[19] See, I am doing a new thing!
    Now it springs up; do you not perceive it?
I am making a way in the wilderness
    and streams in the wasteland.
**Isaiah 43:18-19**

[5] Trust in the LORD with all your heart
    and lean not on your own understanding;
[6] in all your ways submit to him,
    and he will make your paths straight.
**Proverbs 3:5-6**

So do not fear, for I am with you;
    do not be dismayed, for I am your God.
I will strengthen you and help you;
    I will uphold you with my righteous right hand.
**Isaiah 41:10**

What, then, shall we say in response to these
things? If God is for us, who can be against us?
**Romans 8:31**

[1] The LORD is my light and my salvation—
    whom shall I fear?
The LORD is the stronghold of my life—
    of whom shall I be afraid?
[2] When the wicked advance against me
    to devour me,
it is my enemies and my foes
    who will stumble and fall.
[3] Though an army besiege me,
    my heart will not fear;

though war break out against me,
    even then I will be confident.
**Psalm 27:1-3**

In peace I will lie down and sleep,
    for you alone, LORD,
        make me dwell in safety.
**Psalm 4:8**

I can do all this through him who gives me strength.
**Philippians 4:13**

For the Spirit God gave us does not make us timid,
but gives us power, love and self-discipline.
**2 Timothy 1:7**

And my God will meet all your needs according to
the riches of his glory in Christ Jesus.
**Philippians 4:19**

For I know the plans I have for you," declares the
LORD, "plans to prosper you and not to harm you,
plans to give you hope and a future."
**Jeremiah 29:11**

Evening, morning and noon
    I cry out in distress,
        and he hears my voice.
**Psalm 55:17**

I desire to do your will, my God;
    your law is within my heart."
**Psalm 40:8**

No weapon forged against you will prevail,
    and you will refute every tongue that accuses
you...

**Isaiah 54:17**

[38] For I am convinced that neither death nor life, neither angels nor demons, neither the present nor the future, nor any powers,

[39] neither height nor depth, nor anything else in all creation, will be able to separate us from the love of God that is in Christ Jesus our Lord.
**Romans 8:38-39**

And we know that in all things God works for the good of those who love him, who have been called according to his purpose.
**Romans 8:28**

Through you we push back our enemies;
   through your name we trample our foes.
**Psalm 44:5**

He gives strength to the weary
   and increases the power of the weak.
**Isaiah 40:29**

But the Lord is faithful, and he will strengthen you and protect you from the evil one.
**2 Thessalonians 3:3**

The Lord will rescue me from every evil attack and will bring me safely to his heavenly kingdom. To him be glory forever and ever. Amen.
**2 Timothy 4:18**

The LORD is my rock, my fortress and my deliverer;
   my God is my rock, in whom I take refuge,
   my shield and the horn of my salvation, my stronghold.
**Psalm 18:2**

<sup>1</sup> God is our refuge and strength,
    an ever-present help in trouble.
<sup>2</sup> Therefore we will not fear, though the earth give way
    and the mountains fall into the heart of the sea,
<sup>3</sup> though its waters roar and foam
    and the mountains quake with their surging.
**Psalm 46:1-3**

Surely God is my salvation;
    I will trust and not be afraid.
The Lord, the Lord himself, is my strength and my defense;
    he has become my salvation."
**Isaiah 12:2**

You are my hiding place;
    you will protect me from trouble
    and surround me with songs of deliverance.
**Psalm 32:7**

But those who hope in the Lord
    will renew their strength.
They will soar on wings like eagles;
    they will run and not grow weary,
    they will walk and not be faint.
**Isaiah 40:31**

The Lord will fight for you; you need only to be still."
**Exodus 14:14**

The King is enthralled by your beauty! YOU are intentionally and wonderfully made by your loving Creator to uniquely reflect His beauty to the broken world. The busyness and craziness of this world tramples your beauty. Today and every day, you must decide to take care of your hearts, minds, souls and bodies. It's time to step out of feeling unseen, unsought, and uncertain and step into knowing you are INTENTIONALLY and WONDERFULLY MADE!

*¹You have searched me, Lᴏʀᴅ*

   *and you know me.*

*² You know when I sit and when I rise;*

   *you perceive my thoughts from afar.*

*³ You discern my going out and my lying down;*

   *you are familiar with all my ways.*

*⁴ Before a word is on my tongue*

   *you, Lᴏʀᴅ, know it completely.*

*⁵ You hem me in behind and before,*

   *and you lay your hand upon me.*

*⁶ Such knowledge is too wonderful for me,*

   *too lofty for me to attain.*

*7 Where can I go from your Spirit?*

*Where can I flee from your presence?*

*8 If I go up to the heavens, you are there;*

*if I make my bed in the depths, you are there.*

*9 If I rise on the wings of the dawn,*

*if I settle on the far side of the sea,*

*10 even there your hand will guide me,*

*your right hand will hold me fast.*

*11 If I say, "Surely the darkness will hide me*

*and the light become night around me,"*

*12 even the darkness will not be dark to you;*

*the night will shine like the day,*

*for darkness is as light to you.*


*13 For you created my inmost being;*

*you knit me together in my mother's womb.*

*14 I praise you because I am fearfully and*

*wonderfully made.*

Psalm 139:1-14 (NIV)

# intentionally ⊙ yours

10,000 things had to happen for Intentionally Yours to exist...and God arranged each divine moment. From bringing Scott and Sherry to Himself and back to each other after divorce, leading them to share the story of what God had done in their lives, to meeting Rick and Beverly when they were at a crossroads in their marriage. Together, Scott, Sherry, Rick, and Beverly formed Intentionally Yours, to share with every husband and wife that as long as you are breathing, there is hope. Read their stories, hope, and encouragement at www.intentionallyyours.org.

# About Beverly Weeks

Beverly Weeks is an energetic, Jesus-loving "girl-next-door." Her inspiring, transparent messages are seasoned with a little laughter, candid real life struggles, and filled with Biblical truths. Often times people who hear her speak say the same thing, "she's just so real." An evangelist at heart, she has a love for her audience that is fully evident both on and off stage.

Beverly is the Executive Director of a Pregnancy Resource Center, an author, and a speaker. Her greatest joy is being a wife to Rick, and mom to her two children Tyler and Macy.

**Blog/Website:** Dialog with Beverly through her blog post, and follow her speaking schedule. She would love to meet you at an event in your area. www.intentionallyyours.org

**Available For:** Church Events, Women's Conferences & Retreats, Marriage Conferences & Retreats, Banquets, Seminars, and Pregnancy Care Center Events

**Booking Beverly to Speak:** If you are interested in booking Beverly for a speaking engagement, beverly@intentionallyyours.org

Hey Wait a second, who wrote this? I'm just a simple southern girl, tee-totally in love with my Jesus! I love chocolate, peanut butter with bananas, Alfredo sauce, shopping, and consignment shops. Did I say I LOVE chocolate!?

CPSIA information can be obtained
at www.ICGtesting.com
Printed in the USA
FSOW02n2244140416
19199FS